AF324345

You Get to Meet Such Interesting People

To Barb,
We really did
have a great class,
thanks to you

Steve Maurer

You Get to Meet
Such Interesting People

THE ADVENTURES OF AN AMERICAN JOURNALIST

S. P. Maersch

VANTAGE PRESS
New York

Cover design by Sue Thomas

FIRST EDITION

All rights reserved, including the right of
reproduction in whole or in part in any form.

Copyright © 2003 by S. P. Maersch

Published by Vantage Press, Inc.
516 West 34th Street, New York, New York 10001

Manufactured in the United States of America
ISBN: 0-533-14391-8

Library of Congress Catalog Card No.: 2002093343

0 9 8 7 6 5 4 3 2 1

Dedication

Writers write stories, copy editors edit stories. I have read books by journalists who complain about copy editors who "butcher" their prose. Hah! You should see the sausage that passes for journalism in this country. America's newspaper copy editors are holding the whole business together. They are the unsung heroes of journalism, the hard-working grunts who dance on a stage with the curtains closed.

I would like to dedicate this book to, posthumously and humously, my dad, Fred, the funny guy; my mother, Catherine, the poet; my wife, the patient one; and to my wonderful grandsons, Joel and Jimmy. And to Stu Hoyt for going over the manuscript and Rosemary Jensen, who helped with research, and Sherm Gessert, who took my picture.

And I would like to dedicate this work to every journalist and journalist-helper I have ever met in my life. Obviously, I missed a few names. So if you are a journalist who met me and don't mind being named in this dedication, write your name in the space provided at the end of the list. Then you can send me an angry letter and I will send you a book plate you can put in your book.

Carl Fiedler, Chuck Fisher, Harry Maier, A. Matt Werner, Tim Werner, John Werner, Al Nagy, Harley Buchholtz, Lloyd Beining, Frank Barnard, Milf Schreiber, Dwight Pelkin, Marion Koch, Cedric Parker.

Clayton Kirkpatrick, Donald Maxwell, Paul Hubbard, Russell MacFall, Bill Jones, Sara Jane Goodyear, Art Siddon, Bob Nolte, Pat Krizmis, Dane Bath, Bob Corbet, Linda Lee Landis, Larry Fein, Gil Twiss, Bob Finan, John

Stevenson, Bob Dowse, Ron Kotulak, Dennis Gosselin, Wayne Thomis, Eleanor Page, Stephanie Fuller, Tom Fitzpatrick, Ray Walker, Sue Smith, Tom Moore, Joan Pinkerton, Linda Klein, Donna Gill, Chesly Manly, Chuck Mount, Stan Ziemba, Ed Hawley, William Mullen, Casey Bukro, Mitch Dydo, Jim Mateja, Michael V. Smith, Richard Philbrick, George Gunset, Richard Phillips, Pat Terry, Cliff Terry, Sheri Nye, Al Nagelberg, Nick Poulos, Don Gaspar, Lee Fox, Don Starr, Frank Starr, Mike Elliott, Arthur Veysey.

Stu Brown, John Fitzgerald, John Larkins, Bob Millington, Peter Coster, Doug (Stainless) Steele, Peter Fitzgerald, Max Tomlinson, Graeme Kennedy, Neil Town, Maureen Gilchrist, Ann Pilmer, Jill Coutts, Noel Hawken, Belinda Dawson, Tricia Goodwin, Nicholas Columb, John Craven, Jack Elliott, Keith McClure, Elizabeth Hooper, Andrew McKay, Graham Eccles, Jack Cannon, Goeff Clancy.

Dick Leonard, Joe Shoquist, Harry Hill, George Lockwood, Howard Fibich, Tom Barber, Jack Letellier, Pat Horan, John Rammel, Jim Conklin, Steve Hannah, Jeff Browne, Bob Wills, Harry Sonneborn, Malcolm Muggeridge, Harry Pease, Ruth Wilson, Joe Gingery, Arville Schaleben, Avery Witttenberger, Jim Spaulding, Jim Cattey, Bob Sheridan, Jim Oset, Mary Dooley Armstrong, Doug Armstrong, Eric Aspenson, Paul Bargren, Eddie Kaplan, Tom Lubenow, Alex Dobish, Pat Graham.

Dan Chabot, Margo Huston, Valerie Berg, Bob Bestler, Tony Carideo, Malcolm Forbes, Geoff Blaesing, Alan Borsuk, Jeff Britt, Ed Brud, Steve Byers, Christie Cater, Frank Clines, Larry Osman, Linda Maiman, Debbie Wilker, Rob Bessey, Judy Woodburn, Casey Common, Sig Gissler, Sandy Cota, John DeBaun, Alec Dobson, Bill Dowlding, Belle Elving, Ron Elving, Kevin Merida, Anne Curley,

Karen Robinson, Janine Ghelfi, Kim Tondryk, Barbara Baird, Linda Fibich, Bill Fletcher, Terry Folkedahl, Jim Foti, Duane Freitag, Marilyn Frey, Howard Goldfinger, Pat Graham, Dan Hanley, Dave Hendrickson, Nancy Herrick, Mary Beth Jacobsen, Mike Juley.

Ron Leys, Walter Cronkite, Jim Kates, Michele Kenner, Michelle Thompson, Evans Kirkby, John Klein, Ron Kovach, Carroll Kraus, Mike Kuchta, Jim Landers, Ernie Mastroianni, Marilyn Marchione, Bobbi Wahlers, Joann DeWitt, Kathy Naab, Roger Miller, John Mollwitz, Sheila Rockweiler, Pierre-Rene M. Noth, Dominique Noth, Brian Nuedling, Nolan Zavoral.

Marcel Picante, Sue Pierman, Beth Podtburg, Jim Price, Dick Pufall, Pat Reardon, Robert Reichman, Brahm Resnik, Sue Ryon, Paul Salsini, Kathy Schenck, George Schulte, Paul Sevart, Louis Rukeyser, Dulcie Shoener, Jeff Squire, John Stefany, Linda Steiner, Karl Svatek, Barbara Strain, Tom Tolan, Ray Verespej, Don Walker, Mark Ward, John Wells, Bob Wells, Maurice Wozniak, Rich Wronski.

Lois Blinkhorn, Jerry Ziegler, Lynn DiMaggio, Sher Watt, Janet Terrell, Roseann Robertson, Jacci Bates, Susan Spencer Smith, Cheryl Magazine, James Auer, Frank Aukofer, Jan Basina, Fran Bauer, Michael Bauman, David Bednarek, Bill Dwyre, Oliver Kuechle, Carol Matusin, Kevin Lamb, Don Behm, David Behrendt, Drew Pearson, Elizabeth Behrens, Kerwin Berk, Bob Berghaus, Donald Bluhm, Alan Borsuk, Anne Bothwell, Edith Brin, Nancy E. Brome, Paula Brookmire, Ed Mitchell, Don Trenary.

Eric Meyer, Terry Galvin, Vincent Butler, Mary Fran Cahill, Nick Carter, George Cassidy, Dennis Chaptman, Tyler Chin, Thor Christensen, Cliff Christl, Mike Kupper, Terry Bledsoe, Tom Cioni, Regina Clay, Tim Cuprisin,

Nancy Curtis, Dave Daley, Anne Davis, Mike Davis, Barbara Dembski, Carl Schwartz, Matt Devine, Cynthia Dennis, Paul Drzwiecki, Gary D'Amato, Mike Drew, Drew Olson, Joel Dresang, Mark Edmund, Tom Enlund, Darryl Enriquez.

John Fauber, Linda Fausel, Susie Firebaugh, Tom Flaherty, Richard Foster, Elizabeth Francis, Mildred Freese, Mark Gail, Carolina Garcia, Michael Gauger, Erwin Gebhard, Peter Arnett, James Gehrz, Rick Geise, Gene Gerbasi, Dennis Getto, Buck Ryan, Craig Gilbert, Carol Guensburg, Jackie Gray, Donald Griego, Dale Guldan, Erik Gunn, Doris Hajewski, Donald Abert, Cleon Walfoort, Mary Walfoort, Bob Wolf, Evans Kirkby, Bill Letwin, Billy Sixty, Irwin Maier, Tom McCollow, Warren Heyse, Bob Kahlor, Steven J. Smith, Irv Kupcinet, Sherman Gessert, Helen Thomas, Howard Goldfinger, Whitney Gould.

Tom Heinen, Daniel Hanley, Paul Hayes, Bob Helbig, Robert Helf, Elizabeth Hemenway, Mark Hoffman, Andy Horschak, Lynn Howell, Damien Jaques, Patrick Jasperse, April Johnson, Nancy Johnson, Richard P. Jones, Eugene Kane, Richard Kenyon, Meg Kissinger, Greg Klees, Vince Cataruccia, John Kizenkavich, Rosemary Kozak, Joy Krause, Marilyn Krause, Mike Krenn, Clarice Kroening, Annette Lalor, Michelle Landrum, Curtis Lawrence.

Tina Maples, Darryl Ledbetter, Don Lewis, Mark Lisheron, William Lizdas, Deborah Locke, Jackie Loohauis, Tom Lynn, Luis Machare, Don Magarian, Gary Markstein, Sam Martino, Ray McBride, Jessica McBride, Geri McBride, Dennis McCann, Mary McCauley, Bob McGinn, Joel McNally, Mary Jo Meisner, Kathleen Meyer, Ken Miller, Roger Miller, Lois Hagen, Jerry Wilkerson, Jerry Van Ryzin, Bill Manly.

John Mollwitz, Anthony Morales, Bill Nelson, Phil Nero, Mike Nichols, Jack Norman, Tim Norris, Ralph Olive, Jon Olson, Mario Ortiz, Jack Orton, Ronald Overdahl,

Georgia Pabst, Kristin Pelisek, Valerie Phillips, John Pinchard, Barbara Pleva, Wade Mosby, Gary Porter, Jeff Potrykus, Jim Price, Pat Raab, Christine Reed, Jay Reed, Robert Riepenhoff, Marie Rohde, Lori Rondinelli, Neil Rosenberg, James Rowen, Gary Rummeler, Sue Ryon, Chuck Salituro, Paul Salsini, Jo Sandin, Mary Scheffel.

Kathy Schenck, Steve Schultze, William Schulz, John Schumacher, David Schwabe, Paul Sevart, Geeta Sharma-Jensen, Ruth Shattuck, Karen Sherlock, Jennifer Shillinglaw, Joe Shinners, Dulcie Shoener, Amy R. Silvers, Kathy Skiba, Beth Slocum, Jim Slocum, Norah O'Donnell, E. S. Dionne Jr., Jeff Squire, Gregory Stanford, John Stefany, Jerry Steingraber, Jim Stingl, Nancy Stohs, Esther Stolpa, Tom Strini, Lawrence Sussman, Karl Svatek, Leonard Sykes, Charlie Sykes, Janet Terrell, David Thome, Ed Tijerina, David Umhoefer, Tom Vanden Brook.

Ray Verespej, Ned Vespa, Carol Wahlen, Mary Jo Walicki, Don Walker, Laurel Walker, Mark Ward, Sarah Waterman, Joanne Weintraub, Chris Wessling, Becky Williams, Celeste Williams, Bob Wolfley, Richard Wood, Maurice Wozniak, Mike Zahn, Jerry Ziegler, Jeff Zmania, Ken Roesslein, Bob Dye, Jack Thompson, Connie Daniell, Tina Daniell, Diane Bacha, Marta Bender, Tom Mueller, Dave Staats, Pat Rueter, Pat Raab, Peggy Schulz, Charlene Mills, Jim Forrest, Allan Scott, Richard Brodzeller.

Bill Janz, Lisa Polacheck, Jay Joslyn, Dianne Greening, Nancy Raabe, Helen Panly, Larry Engel, Kathleen Waterbury, Jamaal Abdul-Alim, Stan McCoy, Bud Lea, Ken Bunch, Terry Koper, Steve Bruss, Adam Mertz, Josette Cohen, Nancy Beatty, Tracy Harris, Kristina Knapcik, Ella White, Brenda Wolfer, Tony Punko, June Dzemske, Debbie Harings, Terry Olson, Darlene Wimberly.

Jo Reitman, Angie Alexander, Larry Ill, Heather Marshall-Gergen, Lillian Schultz, Marie Spoern, Fayemarie Pluskota, Ruth Ward, Tina Arnold, David Lagerman, Mavis Shoman, Paula Haubrich, David Herron, John Frankland, Linda Randolph, Jim Brandt, Bill Jeske, Marian Rehfeld, Joy Sanasarian, Gail Janke, Annamarie Weiss, Rosemary Jensen.

Melodie Wilson, Kathy Mykleby, Mike Gousha, Mike Jacobs.

Mostert Van Schoor, Gary Brennan, Yogin Devan and Kelly Bostian.

And to ——————————————

—S.P. Maersch, Spring 2003

Contents

You Get to Meet Such Interesting People

1

Harvey Peacock

The story I was editing, by *The Milwaukee Journal's* science writer, Harvey Peacock, was well-written. I had started as a copy editor at The Journal a short time before. I was impressed. There was little to edit. I remember shifting a word and its attendant comma to another location and that was about it. Then I wrote the headline and sent it to the slotman on the desk.

The first edition came off the presses. Everyone in the newsroom got a paper. I saw Peacock clutching his paper and storming toward the copy desk. He looked furious. This could be troub . . .

"What you have done to my story completely changes the thrust of what I wanted to say!" he screamed. "There was no reason to make this change!" He jabbed the paper with his index finger to stress his point. "Why don't you copy editors learn to leave well enough alone!" He continued ranting and raving. He was really hot! I thought he was going to tear out the ceiling tiles and rearrange the fifth floor plumbing. I had never seen anything like this. I leaned back in my chair and thought, "This is what I like about journalism. You get to meet such interesting people."

Peacock's outbursts were legendary. Len Scheller, a copy editor who retired in 1975 (the last copy editor I ever saw who wore a green eye shade), referred to Peacock's outbursts in his retirement speech. He noted the "number of times" he did this and that in his thirty-two years at *The Journal.* "Number of times I gave Marquette T-shirts to Journal staffers and their kiddies . . . six-hundred-seventy-eight." (Or some such number. Len was a real Marquette freak.) Then: "Number of times I changed a story by Harvey Peacock . . . One!"

A reporter told me that Peacock had the view that his story should flow through the editing process as a perfect oblong, like a well-trained Wehrmacht division goose-stepping down Unter den Linden. And if anything were removed from the story, the oblong could be torqued into a parallelogram or, worse, dissolve into complete chaos. This would surely explain Peacock's agitation over the relocated word and its escorting comma.

It was always harder working the Local Copy Desk than the National Copy Desk. On the National Copy Desk you could butcher the prose of the world's best journalists and get away with it. But on the Local Copy Desk the writers were *out there,* like hostile Native Americans, ready to pounce. And pounce they did.

One day Alex Dobish came bounding in from the east. Dobish was a very good writer (his favorite word was "brouhaha"). He was upset over a trim in one of his stories. He broke through two copy desk barricades and got all the way to the news editor. This is roughly like a Comanche attacking Fort Defiance and managing to get inside the sergeant-at-arms' office.

Alex, who was really agitated, got short shrift from the news editor. Then he wheeled about and jumped on the Local Copy Desk slotman. He got no satisfaction there, either. Then, in what psychologists might call a case of misplaced aggression, he unloaded on a copy editor who had nothing to do with the whole thing. No sympathy there, either.

Alex stalked away from the desk. He got about ten feet, turned around and headed back again. He stopped at the rim. "You people have a siege mentality over here, don't you?" he asked. Yep.

After the Peacock Incident, and never wanting anything like that to happen again, I embarked on a study of news room dynamics, of professional courtesies, of ego management, of editor/writer relationships, stuff like that. In the course of my research, I received help from a seemingly unlikely source—Field Marshal Erwin Rommel, "The Desert Fox" of World War II fame. Rommel, military historians like to note, was master of "the diversion." I intended to apply the field marshal's tactics to my job as a copy editor for *The Milwaukee Journal.*

One day I was editing a story by a writer who had a tendency to become hysterical if any of her copy were changed. She was a good writer, but let's face it, even Tiger Woods shanks one now and then. As I edited the story, I came across a paragraph that I felt needed to be altered. I could have made the alteration right there and taken my chances. But I was the shy, withdrawn type and I didn't want to be responsible for visiting Mount St. Helen's II upon *The Journal* news room. So I set that paragraph aside and continued my editing. Then I came across another paragraph that I felt could be changed, but, like, no big deal.

When I finished my editing, I approached the writer. I went to the "no big deal" graph first. "I REALLY THINK this paragraph ought to be changed," I said. "NO!" the writer screamed. "Leave it the way it is!" Then I switched to the primary target. "Well, then, there, now, what about

this graph? Could we change it the way I have suggested
here?" She said, "Well . . . I suppose so!"

Ach ja! Ve make feint at Fezville und capture Tobruk!
Thanks, Erv.

2

The Beginning

Upon receiving my degree from the University of Wisconsin School of Journalism in June 1964, I was to start at the *Milwaukee Sentinel* at $100 a week. That was considered decent money for a journalist in those days. I had interviewed for a number of prospective employers on the campus in Madison, but I figured working in Milwaukee would be nice, and it would be close to my hometown of Sheboygan.

My experience as a journalist at this point was working several summers at the *Sheboygan Press* and also part-time at the *Capital Times* in Madison during one college year. My first news room daddy, Carl Fiedler, city editor of the *Press*, provided me with an unusual reference. He told the *Sentinel* editors that a journalist with my talents was too good for such a newspaper! I interviewed with the *Sentinel*'s Harry Sonneborn and a few other people, one of whom might have been Harvey SchwandNer. Mr. SchwandNer was the Rodney Dangerfield of Milwaukee journalism. Nobody—including journalists, the "get it and get it right" people—seemed able to spell his name right. They always left out the second "n," making him "Schwander." This upset him, but he seemed to take the slight calmly, more so than I would have. I would have jumped on a desk in the Sentinel news room and, like a raging bull, shouted, "All right, alleyez, next one misspells my name's gonna have an N tattooed on his buns!"

Did I say raging bull? That would be Bob (Raging Bull) Wills, probably the finest editor in the *Sentinel*'s

158-year history. (I understand that the paper's founder, Solomon Juneau, was a terrible nitpicker.)

There was a story about Wills in *Milwaukee Magazine* about fifteen years ago written by a former *Sentinel* staffer. (In the article the author misspelled Schwandner!) The author recounted Wills' fabled rantings at his staff, and dubbed him Raging Bull. I was very curious about this. So one day I cornered two Sentinelites at the crosswalk over the Rhine, the alley that separated the *Sentinel* and *Milwaukee Journal* news rooms. "What about this Wills guy?" I asked. "Does he . . . does he really . . . like . . . like, rage?" Their eyes lit up like neon doorknobs and they said, "Oh, yes, he does rage." But they said Wills was a terrific editor who was able to coax the most out of his staff.

I didn't like the way the negotiations went with the *Sentinel.* I wanted to be a copy editor. But they said that since I didn't have any copy editing experience they could start me at only $100. However, I would have to serve a spell as a reporter before being allowed on the copy desk. But I had thirteen-plus months experience as a reporter. They wouldn't credit me with that experience, but they would dock me for my lack of experience as a copy editor. That didn't sit with me too well. So I was relieved when *The Chicago Tribune* called.

It was Clayton Kirkpatrick, assistant managing editor. I had interviewed with Kirk (as everyone called him) on the Madison campus, but was not sure how the interview went, Kirk being the taciturn sort. In preparation for interviews I had whipped together a resume in *Time*-magazine style, cramming it with as many facts about myself as I could. It was only a page and a half long, double-spaced. I figured I would let the interviewers read this while I perused their newspapers and other information they brought to the interview. Kirk asked if he could take my resume with him, and it was the only one I had. I let him take it and wrote another, making copies this time.

I didn't even have my phone number on the resume. Kirk had to get that from the journalism school. Kirk was of the impression that I had been hired by *The Milwaukee Journal*, not the *Sentinel*.

"Would you like to work for the *Tribune*?" Kirk asked. "Yes!" I said. I thought it would be great to get my journalism career underway in a major city, also the only city in America that had four daily newspapers. (The *Tribune* and the afternoon *American* competed with the morning *Sun-Times* and afternoon *Daily News*, the latter two owned by the Marshall Field Co.)

I asked Kirk about pay. "Oh . . . we usually start the new people out at a hundred . . . a hundred ten . . . a hundred twenty. How does that sound?" Hah! That sounded like inflation. I agreed to the $120. He asked me to meet him at the *Tribune*.

I reported this conversation to my journalism counselor, a wonderful old guy named Lester Hawkes, who reminded me of the actor Edmund Gwenn, who played Kris Kringle in "Miracle on 34th Street." Hawkes didn't believe I had been offered that much money until I showed him the letter confirming it. Most graduates that year were getting $100 a week. Hawkes, who was very familiar with midwestern newspapers, said, "Watch Kirk. He's going to be editor of the *Tribune* someday." (Kirk ended up becoming president of the company.) I asked Hawkes about the *Sentinel* situation. Was I in any way obligated to them? After all, I did agree to start there. Hawkes shook his head. "Just write them that you had accepted another offer," he said.

The reaction to my new job varied. Carl Fiedler, city editor of the *Sheboygan Press*, where I had worked during college summers, was pleased. Chuck Fisher, a reporter at the *Press*, felt I had sold out to the right-wing and refused to talk to me. Cedric Parker, city editor of the *Capital Times*, a paper known for its leftist/progressive editorials, shrugged. "The *Trib* is changing," he said.

3

Chicago Days

I took a train to Chicago and walked to Tribune Tower on Michigan Boulevard. I stopped at Kirk's office at the appointed hour and Kirk got out from behind his desk and took me on a personal tour of three floors of the building.

Kirk was a quiet, thinking man, not much given to smiling. He always seemed to be preoccupied with something. He was like a computer. I'm sure if you placed your head close to his you could hear the wheels whirring. Everyone called him Kirk, and he seemed to know everyone. We encountered a scrub lady in one of the hallways. "Good morning, Martha," Kirk said. I was pleasantly impressed. I like editors who say good morning to scrub ladies.

We went up to the fifth floor, where there was an observation deck from which you could gaze down on the huge, two-story tall news room. On the west wall was a huge American flag with the words "America's newspaper for Americans." The McCutcheon poem "Injun' Summer" was on the wall to the right of the flag. On the opposite side were the wire rooms and above them clocks showing the times in various capitals of the world. Most impressive.

The newsroom looked a bit like a gambling casino. The horseshoe-shaped copy desks resembled blackjack tables. There were as many as nine men (no women) on the rims. The slot man sat or stood in the center, looking like the dealer. He would pass out stories to the editors on the rim, then take them back when the editors had finished working on them.

I was anxious to get started. A few weeks later, on what was probably the very day I was supposed to start at the *Sentinel*, I became a *Tribune* man.

Living in Chicago on $120 a week was not easy. I also was $4,200 in debt, counting college loans and a new car I shouldn't have bought. My first few days I stayed at the YMCA on Chicago Street, where I met another Tribune reporter, Chuck Mount, and an Esso employee from Burlington, Wisconsin, Alan Spiegelhoff. We rented a pleasant one-bedroom apartment at Diversey and North Pine Grove. That's how people survived—doubling and tripling up in small apartments. But with all the bills I was paying I felt broke most of the time.

At the *Tribune*, I was assigned to the Neighborhood News Department. There were about forty-five journalists in there, many of them fresh out of college or new to the staff. Neighborhood News turned out zoned sections that ran with the regular edition on Thursdays and Sundays. I was assigned the West Section, covering the city's West Side and the western suburbs. On Thursdays there were four sections—North, West, South and Indiana. On Sundays two more sections, Northwest and South Central, were added.

The *Tribune* started these sections in the 1920s to allow small advertisers to run their ads in a section of the paper that covered just their trading area, and yet run with the big *Tribune*. The sections were preprinted, and our deadlines were three days before printing. This meant we had to produce decent stories that had a three-day shelf-life. Not easy.

On the West Neighborhood News section were Robert (Rapid Robert) Nolte; Sara Jane Goodyear from Watseka,

Illinois; Art Siddon and myself. Art and Sara were dating and a year later got married.

A few weeks after I started, the editors rounded us up into small groups and we were taken to the office of editor Donald Maxwell, who succeeded the fabled Colonel Robert R. McCormick when McCormick died in 1955. Mr. Maxwell greeted us warmly and gave us a pep talk. He welcomed us all into the "*Tribune* Family," said that he didn't care what our political beliefs were, but that as we knew, the *Tribune* was endorsing Senator Barry Goldwater for president that year. He mentioned something about the *Tribune*'s opposition to "creeping socialism," a catch phrase of the day, and he urged us all to do our best.

I was VERY impressed. Here I was, a naïve country bumpkin (well, sort of) from Sheboygan, landing a job on the World's Greatest Newspaper in the only American city with four major dailies. And I was standing in the office of the fabled Colonel Robert R. McCormick and I'm getting a pep talk from the editor himself.

This "*Tribune* Family" stuff might strike some as Betty Crocker-corny, but considering that a writer in Neighborhood News is the lowest form of journalistic life allowed on the paper and that Chicago is an awesome place, this warm welcome by the editor and staff was very important to me and, I presume, to the others. It made us feel special, that we belonged. I thought it was an excellent way to treat the new hirees, and to this day I have warm feelings about it.

I developed a reputation for being a solid writer and a resourceful reporter—a better writer than reporter. We were responsible for producing our own assignments, and I managed to get my share of good stuff. But every now and then editors from what we called the Big Room would come sniffing around. They would go over our news budget and say, "Oh, this is too good for Neighborhood News" and would steal our stories for the daily paper. This happened to my stuff a bit too often, and I have bitter memories of this piracy. We were usually able to replace the pirated stuff with decent stories, but sometimes not.

To thwart the thieves, I tried to develop stories that the Big Room wouldn't want. So I cut back on west suburban news and ventured into the slum areas on Chicago's west side. Chicago's papers did very little reporting on black neighborhoods in those days, so I had a free rein.

When I started at the *Tribune* there was one black journalist there, Eddie Madison, working in Neighborhood News. He soon left for a job in Washington, and the *Tribune* was an all-white operation until 1967, when it hired Joe Boyce. In that year Boyce, after a stint in Neighborhood News, became the first black journalist in the *Tribune*'s Big Room. We took him out to dinner the night before this historic event and asked him how it felt to become the first black on the *Tribune*'s news staff. "I'm scared," he said. I don't blame him. He must have felt incredibly lonely. Boyce was the *Tribune's* Jackie Robinson, and it was not easy for him. There were not just a few racists in the Big Room, I assure you. Boyce went on to have an illustrious journalism career.

I began doing stories about shoddy housing in an area served by groups called the Mile Square Federation and West Side Federation. Blacks were having a tough time finding good housing. They were hemmed in on the east by the expressways and on the other sides by resistant white neighborhoods. Unscrupulous real estate operators were trying to break up the white neighborhoods, buy homes at panic prices, then remodel them into units that they rented to blacks for high prices. The practice of breaking up neighborhoods was called "block-busting," and it could become very ugly. In one neighborhood further south, unscrupulous real estate companies would offer whites "immediate cash" for their homes. In one neighborhood the whites banded together and refused to sell. Block-busters then hired thugs who ventured into the neighborhood and shoved the people's children around as they returned from school. One by one these homeowners sold out, sometimes at panic prices.

The blacks were always having trouble finding decent housing. I toured one slum building where the tenants refused to pay their rent until the landlords did something about the many building code violations. I wrote the story and turned it in to the copy desk. The story was returned immediately with the admonition, "Get the other side!" Damn! I had this beautiful story about people living in a dump and now I had to interview the slumlord and get his side of the story.

The landlord's side was that these people were trashing his properties and he couldn't keep up with the needed repairs. This may have been partly true. I toned down the story considerably and returned it to the copy desk.

Then another copy editor, Tom Carvlin, visited my desk and asked, "Why the mild lede, Steve?" (The lede is the first several paragraphs of a story.) I said, "Well, I had to get both sides and I didn't want it to sound sensational." Carvlin says, "Bullshit." He pulled up a chair, straddled it and motioned me to put some paper in the typewriter. Then he dictated:

"Residents of a rodent-ridden, roach-infested firetrap hope somebody does something about their plight before they all burn to death or are eaten alive by rats."

He took the story and toned it down some, then said, "Bombs away!" and took it back to the copy desk. The landlord ended up paying a modest fine.

While in Neighborhood News I encountered a wonderful copy editor, Pete Negronida, who was to have a profound influence on me. One day I slapped a story together with typos all over the place. I went over the copy, penciling out the misspelled words and typos and writing the correct words above. I turned in the story and headed back to my desk. I didn't even get to sit down when "plop," Negronida dropped the story in front of me. "Retype it," he said. I looked at my story. It was a mess. Then he waggled a finger at me and said, "Professional courtesy." Yes! Professional journalists do not dump trash on the desks of other professional journalists (except at some newspapers).

This incident caused me to change my approach to writing. I could type seventy words a minute, if you don't care about typos. I slowed this to under thirty words per minute and concentrated on accuracy. As accuracy improved, I gradually began increasing my typing speed until it was in the sixties. I began to pride myself with being able to type, at good speed, full pages of copy sometimes error-free, mostly with fewer than three typos. It was a discipline that served me well, throughout my journalism career. It is applicable to the computer as well. If you make an error, correct it immediately. Don't wait until you're done and then go over it. With Pete Negronida's prodding, I became a very clean writer.

Negronida also taught me to respect copy editors. I once went to the desk to complain about a trim made in one of my stories. Negronida took my complaint silently. Then one day he came over to my desk with a story I had written. He pointed to a place where a word was missing, another where I had misspelled a word, another where there was an incomplete sentence. Pete said nothing, but his message came out screaming: "This is what copy editors do for you, so quit complaining about a minor thing like a trim, creep."

The Neighborhood News chief was a jovial, avuncular old-timer named Paul Hubbard. He was a great admirer of the late of Colonel Robert R. McCormick, and his favorite saying was "As the Colonel would say . . . ". We had a lot of fun with this. "As the Colonel would say . . . 'your story smells,'" or, "As the Colonel would say . . . 'the lasagne was wonderful.'" Hubbard soon retired and was replaced by another personable and also avuncular old-timer named Russell McFall. His hobby was gem-polishing, and he wrote books on this subject.

After about a year as a Neighborhood News reporter, I was advanced to the copy desk (women weren't allowed on the copy desks in those days; nor were they allowed to work nights). I got to edit—and nitpick—the stories of other writers and also got a chance to write headlines. I discovered I was reasonably good at this, especially with feature heds. *"Huffing machinery yields crop of fun for Lenox farmer."* (Ugh!) The *Tribune* in these days employed its peculiar spelling of certain words—thru for through, frate for freight, burocrat for bureaucrat. It was fussy about these spellings and reporters had to be familiar with such stylisms before they were allowed on the copy desk as part of their Neighborhood News training. I once wrote a piece of doggerel that I sent to the editor of the *Tribune*'s in-house publication. It went:

As a Tribune copy reader,
I search for consistency.
So, if the word through

He printed it and tendered a humorous reply. About a decade later, the *Tribune* abandoned these spellings.

One day in November 1965 I got "The Call" from Mr. McFall. I entered his office and he motioned me to take a seat. Then he got up from behind his desk, pulled up a chair near mine and plopped his feet on the coffee table. "There's an opening for a copy editor on the National News Desk," he said. "You don't have to take it if you don't want. You can hold out for a writer's position. But as you know, most of these people want to be writers, so you could be waiting for some time. I would advise you to take this." I accepted immediately. And I loved the way he handled it. I now was in the Big Room.

I began work under Larry Fein, a personable and most professional and helpful slotman on the National Desk.

In those days, many newspapers, *Tribune* included, used copy desks as dumping grounds for writers who suffered from various problems, including alcoholism. The *Tribune*'s National Desk was filled with old and often cranky types. I used to joke that when I got up to leave the copy desk the average age of a copy editor rose by fifteen years.

Kirk wanted to change the copy desks. He wanted solid, bright young journalists there. He knew the *Tribune* had a reputation for being stodgy and old-fashioned and he wanted to change that.

Fein taught me a lot about headline-writing, especially in advancing the action of the story. A copy editor named John Stevenson taught me about "bag heds." You write headlines in advance, then when the appropriate story comes along you reach into your bag of pre-written heds and grab the one that fits. Stevenson's favorite bag hed was "Strike looms at textile mill." I never saw that hed in the *Trib*.

The job went well. Once, at the end of a night shift, the slotman said, "Well, Steve, you've had a good night. I'm going to put you down for a day off in the day-off bank." Hey! I can't describe the feeling that came over me. I felt like a three-year-old in potty-training who had just managed his first poopie on the toilet and his parents are standing there applauding.

Editors on the night shift would read the paper carefully, looking for errors, however small. The night managing editor once made a catch that was the talk of the news room for years. He found a wrong-font comma in agate. I always thought there should be awards for such things.

There were a few characters in this newsroom. One was a slotman who worked the overnight shift. He looked like Bela Lugosi. When the second to last edition of the paper would come up we would make changes for the final. On really hectic nights Bela would leap to his feet and stand on his left leg, his right one swaying back and forth like a ballerina prepping for a performance of "Swan Lake."

Then he would pull out a plastic baggie filled with lettuce. His right hand would dart into the bag and, between bites of iceberg and Romaine, he would scream commands at his copy editors. I dubbed this guy "Mac the Lettuce Eater." But after all the changes and corrections had been made, Mac would become the sweetest, most mild-mannered person you could imagine. We would discuss the news of the day, weather, sports, films, whatever. Deadlines do strange things to people.

Another character was the telegraph editor (today we call them national editors.) I used to hear him pitching his news budget to the makeup editor, trying, as all editors do, to win preferable positions for his stories. A typical doping session: "Ahh . . . a bunch of goddam New York shinnies are bitchin' because some of their students are getting beaten up on their way to a rabbinical school. Ahh . . . and there's a bunch of goddam mackerel snappers getting ready for the next ecumenical council."

So Jews were shinnies and Catholics were mackerel snappers and stories about Vietnam war protesters were always slugged "Unwashed." It's amazing how far we've come with this "political correctness" thing.

But if you listened closely to this editor's dopings, you would find that he really didn't like anybody very much. He didn't like blacks, Hispanics, Indians, Orientals—even whites. Nor did he cotton to liberals, moderates or even conservatives. He was one of those truly rare creatures: An equal-opportunity bigot. He retired a while later and at his farewell party fellow staffers poked fun at his salty language. The editor sat there scowling and grumbled, "Why, those c———s———s."

Between editions, *Tribune* staffers liked to hang out at a place called the Boul Mich, just off Michigan Boulevard, where they could catch up on the latest scuttlebutt. ("I hear they're greasing the skids for Charlie.") *Sun-Times* staffers preferred the Radio Grill. The peons from all the papers hung out at the Billy Goat on lower Wacker Drive.

And, brother, did those guys drink! The national and local desk crews would leave for "dinner" after the first edition came out, then return an hour later, some of them inebriated or half way there. Often they ate nothing, just downed a few drinks. I once calculated that the no-return rate for copy editors coming back for the second edition ran somewhere around 3 percent. We gladly covered for the absentees, and I don't know if the managers ever figured out what was happening.

After working the usual hours on the copy desk—2 to 10 P.M., 5 P.M. to 1:30 A.M., 9 P.M. to 5 A.M.—I got the neat job of "early cable man," hours 10 A.M. to 6 P.M. with Saturdays and Sundays off. My job was to set up the foreign news budget, assess the news supplied by our foreign bureaus in London, Paris, Bonn, Tokyo, Mexico City and later Moscow, and take care of the needs of the foreign correspondents and stringers (they were always anxious to get clips of their stories). Among the stringers was David Darrah, a retiree living in Spain. He would produce features for us that we would use in the early editions to hold space for later stories. These anytime features were derisively dubbed "musk ox," to denote their timelessness and also their importance to editors and readers. Darrah's claim to fame was that he was chief of the *Tribune*'s Paris Bureau in 1925 when a young man named William L. Shirer showed up looking for a job. Darrah hired him. Shirer worked for the *Tribune* for about six years, later becoming a member of Edward R. Murrow's CBS radio team in Europe. Shirer wrote such books as *Berlin Diary* and *The Rise and Fall of the Third Reich*. (In 1985 I bought Shirer's book *The Nightmare Years*, in which he recounted his experiences in Nazi Germany. I wrote him about the Darrah thing. Shirer wrote back thanking me and included an autographed book plate.)

One day I cleaned out my desk drawer and found a book of matches. The cover read "Vote for Al Smith. Bring back Bombay Gin." Apparently the desk had not been cleaned since 1928.

In those days, Chicago businesses would throw parties for the media. One of the better parties was dubbed "The Gas Company Gasser." Journalists from all four newspapers were invited. At one of these parties a *Trib-une* staffer was bending over the cheese dip when a huge piece of turkey came flying his way, compliments of the *Sun-Times*. These gassers got to be such unruly affairs that the Gas Company finally gave them up.

Near the center of the *Tribune* newsroom were two raised platforms, about six inches high. One platform contained the desks of the editor, managing editor, news editor and makeup editor. The other platform contained the desks of the national editor, state editor, city editor and foreign editor. By two in the afternoon the newsroom burst into life. The copy desks were manned, the place was filled with reporters, and the *Tribune* began to prepare its first edition for the succeeding day. It was a busy and exciting time. However, the editor, Donald Maxwell, didn't pick up on the excitement. In fact, he often got drowsy.

We copy editors would go down to the composing room to make corrections on our stories before the first edition went to bed. One day Tom Carvlin, now on the Local Desk, was down there. He did a little takeoff on the editor. His eyes wide and glistening, Tom, most dramatically, intoned: "All the desks are manned . . . the writers are writing! . . . the copy editors are editing! . . . The bureaus are filing—Tokyo, Mexico City, London, Paris, Bonn, Moscow—the World's Greatest Newspaper is preparing to go to press! And the editor? He's . . . " and then Carvlin would drop his head, making like a man nodding off.

Shortly after I started on the National Desk, Kirk asked me to dinner at a restaurant in the Wrigley Building. At dinner he asked how things were going, told me about his experiences in London during the war (he loved the theater) and chatted about the problems of afternoon newspapers (difficult to deliver in the rush hour), and said that as a copy editor I would be noticing things I never noticed before and would be "editing" them, like billboards and so forth. Very true!

I didn't know why Kirk had asked me to dinner. I figured he did this with all people new to the Big Room, I didn't make a big deal out of it and I didn't tell anyone about it until a year later. "What!" they exclaimed. "Kirk never takes ANYONE to dinner."

Kirk was doing to the *Tribune* what Pope John XXIII said he was doing with the Catholic Church. He was opening windows to let some fresh air in the place, and pushing the *Tribune* into a new era. He did a fantastic job of this. And I got the impression that perhaps Kirk wanted me to become one of the new, young editors to help in this endeavor. It is truly pleasant to think so. If it were true, I was to disappoint him.

In November 1967 a terrible thing happened in my life. I turned thirty. It was a traumatic event for me, and I began to reassess my life and figure out what I wanted to do with it. I asked myself whether I wanted to work at the *Tribune* the rest of my life, and I concluded no, I was all thru. I had long been an admirer of *Time* magazine and wanted to work there. So I dashed off three job applications: to *Time* magazine, to CBS, and, more or less for insurance, the *Chicago Daily News*. *Time* said they couldn't take me on their staff, but I could work for them free-lance. I did a story for them, on dog food. They never asked me to do another, so I guess they weren't very impressed. When I checked my story in the magazine I could find only one sentence that I could call my own. CBS sent a polite no thanks. But the *Daily News* said it was definitely interested and asked me to come over for a tryout.

I sneaked into Chicago on several Saturday mornings to take the *Daily News* test. I passed. A couple days later, while I was working on the *Tribune*'s National Desk, I got a call from the slotman on the *Daily News*. "We want you to work for us. We can offer you $220 a week." He said this proudly, as though he knew I was making considerably less. Wow, I thought. That's big bucks. The *Trib* had just raised me to $185 in October. So $220 would be a raise of almost 20%. But it was juicier than that. The *Daily News* had a night differential of 10%, and I would be working the overnight shift so I would be getting $242 a week. However, by this time I was getting wise to the salary game, so I told the slotman, "Make it $230 and you've got your man." He seemed annoyed, said he'd have to check with the managing editor. He called back a few minutes later and said, "OK, it's $230." With the 10 percent night differential that would come to $253. I put in my three weeks notice. The *Tribune* asked me to reduce it to two weeks, which I did, and I used the third week to take a trip to New York.

So I was making $185 at the *Tribune* and now would be making $253 at the *Daily News*—a 37 percent increase in pay.

Kirk, by now executive editor, wanted to know what happened. I told him, "They offered me so much money I couldn't possibly turn it down." I wish I had been more specific. I liked Kirk. He was the finest editor I ever worked for, and in a way I felt like his protégé. I thought I was a bit like him personally.

Larry Fein, slotman on the National Desk, also wanted to know what happened. We took a walk down Michigan Boulevard. He told me he was sorry to see me leave because I was one of only two copy editors he had who could turn a bright hed.

I quaffed a few at the Boul Mich with Jim Kirby, chief of the Local Copy Desk. He asked, "Why are you leaving the *Tribune* after all these years, Steve?" And I said, "Well, basically, it's sixty-eight more bucks a week." He says, "Hell, I don't blame you. I'd leave, too." Then he told me that in the 1930s he was working on a paper in Michigan. The paper was sold to a chain. The managing editor gathered the staff in the news room, jumped on a desk and said, "Now don't anybody worry. The new owners have promised that you'll all keep your jobs." Kirby says, "I didn't believe that, so I went down to Indiana and got a job at a paper there. When I came back, the managing editor saw me and says, 'Where have you been?' I said, 'I didn't believe that stuff about our jobs being safe here, so I went down to Indiana and got a job on a paper there.' And the managing editor said, 'Oh, yeah? Are they still hiring? I just got laid off.' "

The "sixty-eight more bucks a week" remark spread through the *Tribune* news room like wildfire. Then Tom Moffatt, a young new copy editor, jumped to the *Sun-Times*. Then another young copy editor jumped across the street. Kirk was upset. He had been hiring young people to staff his copy desks to replace the old fogies, and now his young Turks were not only leaving the *Tribune*, but were getting jobs at the hated Field newspapers. If newspapers covered their own newsrooms (which they don't) there was a story here, and I have a *Tribune*-style hed for it: "Kirk's de-geezerization plan imperiled."

A year later a *Tribune* staffer told me that Kirk's reaction was immediate and dramatic. He said Kirk ordered $20 a week raises for his copy editors, then set up a committee to study pay differences between the *Tribune* papers and Field papers. After that, he ordered another raise for the desk people, I believe $15.

When I applied at the *Daily News* I billed myself as "The World's Greatest Copy Editor" after the *Tribune*'s slogan "World's Greatest Newspaper." The managing editor, Daryl Feldmeir, thought that was clever. It also was an incredible exaggeration!

The *Daily News* was a much smaller and tighter paper than the *Tribune*. I found that the *Daily News* copy editors would check names in their writers' copy against those in the *Tribune*. The *Tribune* had a reputation for getting names right.

The *Daily News* had a great stable of writers, including Keyes Beach, Peter Lisagor and the fabled Mike Royko. One night we heard a burst of laughter across the newsroom. Royko's column had just been filed, and an editor was going over it. He stopped at the copy desk to read it to us. Can't recall it exactly, but it went something like this:

A letter from a fighting man to his parents back home.

Dear Mom, Dad, Sis and Spot.

We're completely surrounded by the enemy. Don't know how long we can hold out. Our food ran out yesterday, and now they're going to shut off our water.

Perhaps we shouldn't have seized the dean's office in the first place. But you didn't raise your son to be a coward.

And the column went on about a campus sit-in.

Nineteen sixty-eight was a rough year. Martin Luther King Jr., assassinated. Robert F. Kennedy, assassinated. Cities were rioting. My old stomping grounds, the Mile Square Federation area, went up in flames. I drove through the area later. It was like driving through a mouth full of rotted and missing teeth.

The Democratic National Convention, held in Chicago, was a violent mess. It inspired Mayor Richard J. Daley's tortured quote: "Da job a da police is not to start disorder. Da job a da police is to preserve disorder." I was beginning to dislike Chicago. Living in big cities can be a hassle. One day, while with the *Tribune*, I came to work and noticed a trail of blood leading from the subway platform out to the street at the Grand Avenue stop. A passenger had been stabbed, I believe fatally, on a subway train. Our bosses at the *Tribune* told us to travel home in groups. I talked to the people in our group. Most had had unpleasant experiences on the elevateds. I told them I had never had any trouble. "That's because you look like a cop," they said.

The *Daily News* faced an uncertain future, which was why it had to pay top dollar to get people to work there. The paper, which owned a huge pile of Pulitzers, went out of business seven years later.

In late 1968 I decided I was through with working in Chicago and perhaps in big cities generally. It was time to move on.

I truly believed in Thoreau's utterance, "The mass of men lead lives of quiet desperation." (Tut-tut, Thoreau! You should have said "leads," since "mass" is singular. Goes to show, even Thoreau could have used a copy editor!) I felt that age thirty marked the beginning of the end of my life, and I wanted to do something first. I decided to do something I had wanted to do since serving in the Navy in 1957 and 1958: Take a trip around the world.

I wrote to the Maritime Administration to get a transcript of sea service. I was credited with twenty-one months sea duty. (I had served on a tanker in the Mediterranean-based 6th Fleet). I used this to get a U.S. Coast

Guard Merchant Mariner's Document—a seaman's card. This would qualify me for a job on a U.S. merchant ship.

Then I wrote the editors of several papers in Australia, asking if they could take an American on their staff for a while. I got a reply from Stu Brown, editor of the *Melbourne Herald*, saying, yes, they could use a Yank on their staff for a few months. He said the pay wouldn't be much (about $110 U.S.) but I would have a few bucks left over for "grog," as they call liquor. I wrote him to expect me in January or early February 1969.

My plan was to make one trip on a merchant ship in the Pacific, then head down to Australia for a few months and continue my trip around the world from there. I didn't have a solid itinerary laid out, but I wanted to travel by surface as much as possible to get an idea of the size of the world. I would make plans as I went along.

In October I gave the *Daily News* my notice. After farewell parties in Sheboygan and Chicago, I left. Carrying a hundred pounds of gear, I boarded a train in Chicago for San Francisco.

4

Pacific Adventure

First thing on arriving in San Francisco I went to the Seafarers International Union hiring hall. (The Seafarers Union, oddly enough, represented Chicago's cab drivers). I walked up to the desk and presented my seaman's card to a kindly looking old man and said, "I would like to get a job on a ship."

The man looked over the card to assure himself it was genuine, and asked, "Ever been to sea before?"

"In the Navy," I replied. "Not the merchant marine."

The man grumbled something about "first-trippers," turned to a file and pulled open a drawer. "All these guys are ahead of you," he said. "They're from our training school, and we place them on ships first. You can wait if you want, but it could take a long time. Even months."

There must have been 150 cards in that drawer. They were among the so-called "entry ratings," those going to sea for the first time as ordinary seamen, wipers or messmen. So there I was, with a seaman's card, but with dim prospects of getting a job on a ship. It was now October, the *Melbourne Herald* wasn't expecting me until January or February, so without a job on a ship I would have a lot of time to kill. There were other unions, such as the Sailors Union of the Pacific and the National Maritime Union, but I never tried there.

I hashed over my alternatives. I scanned the San Francisco newspapers looking for work to keep me going before leaving for Australia in January, and I arranged for two job interviews.

Then I ran into a salesman from Los Angeles who told me the Seafarers Union was running the Hubert Humphrey-Edmund Muskie presidential campaign headquarters on Mission Street I went over there. The headquarters was a former furniture store decorated in red, white and blue and equipped with all the stuff of presidential campaigns: desks, chairs, and tables with rows of phones and all the usual campaign paraphernalia—pamphlets, buttons, brochures, signs.

A Humphrey-hatted greeter met me at the door. I told him what I wanted. He said the man to see was a union vice president. "He'll be in in an hour," he said. I waited.

A man rushed inside and made his way to an office in the rear of the headquarters. The Humphrey-hatted greeter nodded and I followed the man to the office. I slinked into a chair while the official talked on the phone. As soon as he hung up and before he had a chance to dial again, I told him I would be willing to work at the headquarters for free until election day if the union could get me a job on a ship. "We could never make a deal like that," he said. "However, if you would like to volunteer some time . . . "

I left dejected, but determined to get a job on a ship.

I put in a few conspicuous hours as a campaign volunteer. Then I drafted a new proposition and returned to the headquarters in the afternoon. This time I captured the ear of the union's legal secretary, who was acting as the barn boss at the Mission Street office. I gave him the same story I had given the union veep. I told him I was a Humphrey supporter (I actually favored Eugene McCarthy) and said I would work 100 hours in the two weeks till the election if they would get me a job on a ship after the election. If they couldn't deliver on a deal like that, they would be out 100 hours of free labor. The man's eyes widened, and after I finished he disappeared into the office to talk to the very union vice president who had turned me down earlier. He was back in two minutes. "You've got your ship," he said. There was more good news: The union would pay me $50 a week for my work (they finally paid me $150) and would waive the $35 fee for a physical exam at a union clinic. Marvelous!

My job in the Humphrey headquarters was to supervise up to thirty phone callers as they tried to contact every voter in San Francisco to give the Humphrey-Muskie spiel. I made several hundred phone calls myself.

One day the union official running the place asked me to take his car to fetch some campaign literature. His car was a big, four-door job. One of my favorite films is *Bullitt*, filmed that year, in which Steve McQueen jumps into his Mustang and goes leaping around San Francisco's streets after a pair of baddies.

Well, I'm no Steve McQueen. I got into that big sedan and started driving the streets of San Francisco. I was petrified. I would drive down one of those steep streets and stop at an intersection. I could not see the street in front of me over the car's hood. All I could see was the next intersection. I glanced about to make sure nobody was looking. Then I got out of the car and walked forward to make sure there indeed was a street in front of me. Then I got in and drove again. I felt like an idiot, but . . .

One day I hopped one of the city's cable cars and failed to pay the forty-five cent fare. So I sent forty-five cents to the Public Utilities Commission. I got a nice thank-you letter—and a mention in Herb Caen's column in the *San Francisco Examiner*!

The barn boss wanted me to put in eight hours every day until the election. I did, but managed to extricate myself for a weekend in Los Angeles and Beverly Hills.

My brother Philipp's wife, Patty, had relatives in Hollywood (not movie stars) and I spent a weekend with them. They took me on a tour of stars' homes.

Many of the "volunteers" in the office were graduates or students of the training school who were putting in time, under coercion, probably, before getting jobs on ships. There also were a handful of "first-trippers" like myself. Many of these men were not young. They were guys running away from bad marriages, or unpleasant situations. They were guys like myself—misfits, drifters, veterans, oddballs, hippies (which one Hispanic union official called "heepies"). In some ways, the merchant marine serves as America's French Foreign Legion.

Humphrey and Muskie lost the 1968 election, but carried the city of San Francisco seven votes to four, thanks to our help.

The day after the election I returned to the headquarters and helped disconnect phones and carry out furniture. I "ahemed" a union officer and gave him a look that said, "You haven't forgotten about our little deal, have you?" He called the hiring hall, asked for a man named Tom, gave him my name and hung up. "Go down to the hiring hall and get a card for your physical," he said. "When you're finished with the physical you wait two days to see that everything is all right. Then you pick up your clinic card, return to the hiring hall and we'll ship you out."

The physical took three hours. The doctor joked, "You're not in such awful shape for a man your age." I had turned thirty-one the day before.

A day later I went to the clinic to get the medical certification card. A nurse shuffled through the card pile on the desk. Mine was not there. "You'll have to wait a while, sir," the nurse said. "The doctor wants to see you."

Eyes. Five years earlier they were good enough to get me assigned to Navy Officers' Candidate School in Bainbridge, Maryland. I wasn't serious about becoming a Navy officer; I was just curious if I could qualify. Now my eyes were not good enough for a job as an ordinary seaman. The doctor stamped the card STEW'D DEPT. ONLY and sent me on my way.

I went back to the union hiring hall and gave my card to a dispatcher, who happened to be the same Humphrey-hatted greeter I had met on my first visit to the headquarters. By this time I knew him well.

"Sit over there and wait awhile, Steve," he said. Wait, wait, wait. This was getting to be like the Navy. Two and a half hours passed. And at exactly 1:35 P.M. on Nov. 8, 1968, my name and that of my ship were uttered in the same breath.

"Steve," the dispatcher shouted. "Your ship is the *Tucson*. It's in the Willamette shipyards. Go down to the Overseas Medical Center and get your shots, then pack your gear and get on board. You'll get paid for today."

I was so delighted I forgot to look at the white card telling me what my shipboard duties would be. I was classified as a "galley utility." Yep, a messman. This was beginning to look like something out of a Jack London tale.

There was still more waiting. I walked over to the Overseas Medical Center on California Street and gave my name to the receptionist. I underwent yet another physical.

After that I was ushered into a room where a nurse stood before a row of needles intended for me. She instructed me to roll up my left sleeve. As she swabbed the arm she said, "You're going to Vietnam, huh?" I told the nurse I had no idea where I was going. I was getting inoculations for smallpox and cholera and shots for typhoid, tetanus, typhus and plague. "Yes," the nurse said, "you're going to Vietnam."

The Willamette shipyards were in Oakland. I don't remember much of Oakland, so Gertrude Stein probably was right, there is no *there* there. I found the *Tucson*. It actually was the *Tucson Victory*, a World War II Victory ship put in the reserve fleet at the end of the war, then demothballed in 1966 for duty on the Vietnam run. The ship looked awful. Even the name on her bows was partly obliterated by rust.

The ship was operated for the U.S. government's Military Sea Transportation Service. It was of the usual drab military colors—deck gray, haze gray, black and white—except for the rust. I learned that there were 172 Victory ships in service on the Vietnam run. The Victories were well built, with turbine engines that could deliver about sixteen knots. In World War II the U.S. also built thousands of Liberty ships, which had reciprocating engines that could produce only eleven knots. The Liberties were scrapped after the war, but the government hung on to the Victories, just in case.

It took me two trips to lug all my gear up the gangway. In the galley I found the steward, who would be my boss. He said, "You've got the officers' mess (dining room). Ya kin go ashore now, but be sure yer back at 6 A.M. to go to work."

Then the steward turned and asked, "Where's Fred at?" A man with an enormous belly appeared. The steward said, "Fred here'll show ya yer bunk."

I followed Fred down the passageway on the port side. We came to the end of it and and he pulled out a key and unlocked a door with the number 26 on it.

"Heeyuh," he said in a Brooklyn accent. "Dis is yor bunk. Ovuh thayuh's yor lockah."

The compartment contained an upper and lower bunk and two lockers on one side and a single bunk and locker on the other. In between was a porthole. The only furniture was a battered writing table. I was assigned the lower bunk, but was soon to get the single bunk when Fred left the ship. He, like a few other crewmen, didn't want to go to Vietnam.

The bunks could rate the description "beds," because they had innerspring mattresses. Not exactly plush, but certainly better than I had been accustomed to in the Navy, where we got one thin slab of a mattress and one woolen blanket.

The base pay for an officers' messman was $302 a month. But there was automatic overtime for Saturday and Sunday work, which added sixteen more hours' pay at $1.89 an hour. There also was so-called "port time" worth three hours overtime each day the ship was in a U.S. port. There were three meals a day, three entrees on the menu, all you can eat and very good.

After seeing the condition of the ship I was glad I was a messman instead of a deck seaman. My duties included bringing the officers their meals three times a day and keeping their mess area clean. The officers proved easy to get along with and interesting to talk to, especially the engineering officers, who for some reason seemed more cerebral and conversational than the deck officers. The officers were, almost to the man, farsighted. Some would hold the menu out front as far as possible and still could hardly read it. I suppose this was a product of their vocation, since they spent so much time peering at things distant.

In my first several days aboard the ship I clambered over everything to find out what I could about her. She was 455 feet long, 62 feet wide, drew 31 feet of water loaded, weighed 7,607 tons gross. There were three cargo holds forward of the bridge and two aft. There were cargo booms and winches at each hatch.

An architect's sketch noted that she was built in California in 1945 and whoever drew the diagram misspelled the ship's name "Tuscon Victory."

On Nov. 16 the ship's destinations were posted: Seattle, Bangor, Subic Bay, Da Nang. We were to pick up shoring equipment in Seattle. Bangor was a huge ordnance depot north of Seattle. Subic Bay was a big Navy base in the Philippines. Da Nang was in Vietnam. Our cargo would be 30,000 bombs, mostly 500-pounders, some 1,000-pounders. Detonators would be carried in crates on the deck.

We left Oakland on November 17, slipped under the Golden Gate Bridge and headed north to Seattle. The seas were choppy and I got seasick almost immediately. I would always get sick at the start of a voyage, then get over it. The officers got sick too, and I noticed quite a few of them failed to make it to meals when we first got underway. The captain said at dinner one evening that about 5 percent of people don't get seasick, 90 percent get seasick and shake it, and a most unfortunate 5 percent get seasick and don't get over it. He advised sufferers never to lie down. Stay on your feet and you will get your sea legs, he said — unless, of course, you are among the unfortunate 5 percent.

In Seattle, the *Tucson Victory* began rounding out her crew. An able-bodied seaman was flown in from Boston. From Denver came a messman, and from Michigan an engineering officer. In four days the ship had enough officers and men to receive the approval of the shipping commissioner to make a voyage.

The officers who would run the *Tucson Victory* were the master (captain), first (or chief) mate, second mate and third mate. In the engineering department was the chief engineer, first assistant, second assistant and third assistant. Then there was Sparks, the radioman.

The ship had a bosun (boatswain), deck maintenanceman, six able-bodied seamen, and three ordinary seamen. The engineering department had a chief and a second electrician, three oilers, three firemen-water tenders, and two wipers. In the steward's department were the steward, chief cook, baker-second cook, third cook, four messman (I was one), a pot and pan washer and a compartment cleaner. Forty men in all.

The merchant marine has a lingo of its own. It's sometimes called "the merch." Officers are addressed by rank, sometimes in strange combinations, as in "Just a second, Third."

There were a few Orientals and Filipinos who would just DIE without their rice, a onetime bit actor (*Hell Is for Heroes*), several skid-row types, no blacks although the Seafarers Union has many.

We crewmen had to sign shipping articles valid for a year or until the ship would again reach port in the continental United States.

There would be a 10 percent increase in pay with the first loading of the bombs. Once the ship was within 100 miles of Vietnam (war zone) pay would double, plus the 10 percent differential for the bomb cargo. If the ship were hit by enemy fire (a not uncommon occurrence, I was told), each crewman would receive $300 for each incident.

The second engineer told me that several bomb ships had been sunk in Vietnamese waters, but the government kept the news quiet. Merchant seaman serving on Vietnam-bound ships were entitled to a Vietnam Service bar. (I have mine.)

The *Tucson Victory* was a lady with a propulsion plant of questionable virtue. She was classified as a "tramp steamer." She showed she couldn't be on time if she wanted to. On occasion, because of engine problems, she made little more than four knots.

Bangor was a short distance from Seattle. We hardly got our mooring lines over when men in rain coats and hard hats swarmed aboard, the hatches were opened and we began loading our cargo.

The first mate scurried about the ship posting signs: "Do not carry matches or lighters," and "Smoking in crew's and officers' lounges only." The restrictions went unheeded. Boxcars on the dock were opened, and the bombs, in crates of six, were carefully forklifted to the pier.

The ship's loading gear took over, and there followed the groaning and whump-whump of the winches, interspersed with the blowing of whistles as the bombs were lifted from the dock and gently eased into the holds. Forklifts nudged the crates into their assigned places and workmen shored up the crates to make sure they would not move. A cargo shift could be disastrous.

More bombs waited on barges out in the bay, red pennants warning of the dangerous cargo.

The 500-pound bombs were about four feet long and nine inches in diameter. They were painted olive drab and had yellow nose covers with olive-drab tips. The bombs were stacked almost to the tops of the holds.

Where they were stowed end-in, their tips peered outward like so many menacing eyes.

It took only three 500-pound bombs to destroy the Japanese aircraft carrier Akagi in the Battle of Midway during World War II. I wondered what 30,000 such bombs could do. If each bomb killed just three people, I was helping to deliver 90,000 deaths. I was not proud of that.

Loading went on from early morning until 1 A.M., interrupted by frequent and severe rain squalls that sent the men scurrying for shelter.

On the fifth day the whump-whump and the groaning of the winches and the blowing of the whistles stopped, to be replaced by the pounding of hammers as the workers shored up the last of the bombs and built wooden framework around deck cargo on either side of the No. 4 hold. A catwalk was constructed over that cargo on the starboard (right) side, and a stairway was built up to it.

The hatch covers were clamped into place and heavy, dark-colored tarpaulins were draped over each hold and secured to the sides with wooden wedges pounded in by sledge hammers. Then the pounding and tap-tapping stopped, the swarm of men disappeared and the ship was silent.

There were several other Victory ships in port with us. One of them, the *Lynn Victory*, left but straggled into port a day later with engine problems. It seemed that the engineers were having a terrible time coaxing these quarter-century-old engines to perform properly.

Our sailing time was set for 1430 (2:30 P.M.) Wednesday, November 27. The ship first anchored in the bay so engineers could conduct final tests on the engines. Then, four hours late and with a slight list to port, the *Tucson Victory* drew up anchor and began her voyage to Vietnam.

The winds howled and the seas snarled angrily as the ship headed into a Pacific storm. We began rolling twenty, then thirty degrees. I had shaken my seasickness a long time ago and now was having fun. Delivering plates of food to the officers' mess was a challenge. I would get two plates of food in the galley, just below the mess room. I would then enter the stairwell and lean backwards against a starboard bulkhead as the ship rolled right. As the ship began to level off, I would scramble up the stairway and at the top would lean backwards against a port bulkhead as the ship rolled left. As the ship leveled off again, I would rush inside the officers' mess and put the plates on the table. I would hang onto a table till the ship finished its roll right, then race out and clamber down the stairs to get two more plates. The captain bawled me out for not wetting the table cloths to keep the plates from sliding. I didn't know I was supposed to do that. (In the Navy we would put a piece of bread under our trays to keep them from shifting).

The ship was on a south-southwesterly course. If she were to take a more direct route to Subic Bay she would be in the far North Pacific, on a so-called Great Circle Route. But the far North Pacific is exceptionally stormy in November, and for a ship like the *Tucson Victory*, with bombs as cargo, a calmer, more southerly route was ordered. This would be a voyage of about 7,000 miles.

Even while on the southern route, the ship kept as far as 500 miles from the usual sea lanes to minimize the danger of collision. And because of the warlike nature of the ship's mission, the radioman was ordered to divulge the course to no one.

By nightfall the clinometer on the bridge was registering rolls of more than thirty degrees. Everything movable was lashed down, and crewmen were ordered to stay clear of open decks. During the early hours of the morning the ship took a series of severe rolls. There was a crunching sound, which I took to be (and which probably was) the ship hitting a wave broadside, then a tip-tip-tip-tip WHOOSH, followed by the noises of things toppling over that shouldn't be toppling over. There were cries of "Hey, hey!" from crewmen being hurled about, and shouting from the engine room where a paint drum had broken loose and spattered its contents over a wide area. No one could sleep. We had to hold on just to keep from being thrown from our bunks.

I struggled to the officers' mess, where I found the third mate, who had just got off watch. "How big were the rolls?" I asked.

"More than forty degrees," he said.

"Could we take a fifty?"

"Yes, but the booms would probably go."

"How about a sixty?"

"You probably wouldn't be around long enough to worry about it," he said.

The biggest roll I had experienced up to this was thirty-five degrees, while on a Navy ship in the Mediterranean. Our biggest roll this night was forty-two degrees. If you were trying to walk down a passageway during one of those rolls you would have one foot on the deck and the other almost equally on a bulkhead.

By morning the seas had subsided some and the captain ordered the ship hove to (stopped) to check for damage. A ventilator had been bashed in, and the catwalk over the cargo hatch had been torn away. The waves also had begun to chew away at the planking on the deck cargo. The decks were awash with pieces of wood and other debris torn loose in the fury of the night. The wood looked like it had been chewed by teeth.

Suddenly a scream. "Look at that! Look at that!" I looked astern and my jaw dropped. Approaching from the stern was a mountain of water—we estimated it at forty feet—approaching the ship. I grabbed something and hung on. I thought this was it. The stern lurched upward violently and we went up, up, up, up and then down again. Apparently we bobbed over this huge wave like a cork. It must have been one of those "rogue waves" that are created by storms. I didn't like this at all. When something like this happened I thought, "I must have a death wish."

Damage repaired, the ship got underway again, pushing its way through a valley of large, bobbing, blue and green hills. An awesome sight.

We were fortunate to survive the storm with so little damage. Two months later a ship just like ours encountered a similar storm and its bomb cargo broke loose. The crew could not secure the bombs and more and more broke loose and tumbled around in the holds, banging against the hull. The captain ordered the crew to abandon ship. As a life boat was being lowered, bombs broke through the hull and landed on the boat, killing several men. About half the crew perished in that incident.

I got along with the officers and crew fairly well. I received only one death threat. An ex-boxer from Mississippi vowed to kill me as soon as we got to Subic Bay. He hung a punching bag in his compartment and drew a crude likeness of me on it. The way he attacked that thing gave me the creeps. I didn't know whether to take the death threat seriously or not. Perhaps not, since I am still alive. But I can tell you that these ships were crewed by some mean, unstable and strange people. Count me in. The second engineer said this crew was a rough bunch, but that he had seen worse in his twenty-four years at sea. He said some ships even had ex-cons among the officers.

I calmed down the angry boxer (I still don't remember what he was angry about) by helping him write letters home. I believe he was illiterate (maybe that's how I offended him!) I would type entire paragraphs without direction, then read them to him and ask if they were OK, and he would nod, "Yah."

On Dec. 7, I put a note in a bottle along with the *Tucson Victory*'s longitude and latitude, which I got from the third mate. I enclosed a dollar bill, sealed the bottle and tossed it over the side. The note contained my address in the States and offered the finder $10.

(In June 1971 I received a letter from a Juan T. Turado, a forestry student from Caloocan City, Philippines. He said he was fishing at six o'clock on the morning of June 6, 1971, when "I saw your bottle floating on the big waves in the ocean and because of cureousity [sic], I got it." He sent me a xeroxed copy of the message in the bottle! I was delighted to send him his $10. I wrote the National Oceanic and Atmospheric Administration about this and they said it was very unusual for a bottle to be found after such a long time at sea. But they said that a bottle released by Boy Scouts off Savannah, Georgia, was found seven years later on a Florida beach north of St. Petersburg.)

The trip from Bangor to Subic Bay was to take about nineteen days. But the *Tucson Victory*, acting like an old mare who wanted to be put out to pasture, broke down several times, and these problems, along with the storm, added three days to the trip.

The captain, an old geezer named L. J. Hubbard, was a gruff fellow, but thoroughly approachable. He had a tough job. One day he commented on the beard I was growing. He said shave it off or let it grow. I spent days stroking my beard wondering what my third alternative was.

The crew's messmen, Mike and Pee Wee, were known as "The Kids." They would prance around the ship like a pair of puppies, getting into all sorts of mischief. A victim of many of their high-jinks was a jug-eared, good-humored Irishman we dubbed "Jack the Wiper." The Kids would poke Jack and try to get him to whistle, but since he had lost his dentures the only thing he could manage was a "Pfffft!" In Subic Bay Jack picked up a new set of dentures, and while he never became known as "Jack the Whistler," he now could manage at least a little tweet.

One of my favorite books is *Mutiny on the Bounty*. I like that scene where the H.M.S. *Bounty* drops anchor at Tahiti and the natives paddle to the ship in their outriggers. Almost two centuries later, same thing. As we entered Subic Bay the natives came rushing to greet us in their outriggers. But these were large boats with outboard motors. They knew we had cigarettes and they were eager to trade. Their boats were loaded with cases of beer, bottles of liquor and other goodies.

A great deal of trading ensued off the stern of the ship. Crewmen would wave their cigarette cartons in the air, and the natives would hold up the appropriate number of fingers indicating that a deal had been made for cases of beer. Then the cartons would be tossed into the boats and there would be a furious tugging of ropes as the cases of beer were hauled aboard. We pulled more than 100 cases of beer into that ship, plus many bottles of booze. All this was illegal, of course, but did I see Captain Hubbard looking the other way? For five cartons of cigarettes I got two cases of beer, two bottles of rum and a bottle of gin. I thought I had done quite well.

We were anchored well out in Subic Bay (harbormasters don't like bomb ships in port) and lighters were sent out to take off about half our bombs to a huge ammo depot that the U.S. Navy operated there. A sign on a watch tower at the depot warned that all radio and radar transmitters had to be shut down to eliminate the danger of setting off variable-time ammunition, whose detonators contained sensitive radio devices.

We got to take liberty in the city of Olongapo. Russ, my partner in the officers' mess and I hired an outrigger to take us in. The ride was wild and wet. I could not believe I was doing this.

Olongapo was a strip of bars, nightclubs, bawdy houses, clip joints, and hotels where seamen were happily relieved of their money for favors of various sorts. We visited a nightclub where a good band was playing a version of "Hey, Jude." That became the theme song of our ship. The Filipino beer was very good.

In Subic Bay I learned how different the merchant marine was from the U.S. Navy. Some of the crewmen would take off for days. Some never returned. Russ vanished for a day, and there was a rumor that he had been shot. But he returned, then I took off for two days. When I returned the captain warned me that I did not have the steward's permission to do that, but by this time the cook and several others had taken off.

After six days in Subic Bay the *Tucson Victory* prepared to sail. A nose count showed two men had vanished and another crewman had become ill. That left the ship with thirty-seven of its original forty crew. We hauled anchor on December 28 and headed for Da Nang. The seas were calm.

As we entered the bay of Da Nang the warm stench of land struck our nostrils, replacing the cool freshness of the sea air. In the purple brown hills that surrounded the bay we could see fires burning and hear an occasional explosion. The air was smoky. Now and then a plane would fly over, and were those 500-pound bombs attached to the wings? At night we saw tracer bullets scooting from hill to hill and heard explosions and other sounds of war.

A contingent of Coast Guard and Navy men came aboard to supervise the unloading and to guard the ship against attack. There was a rumor of a rocket attack to come from a pier only 300 yards away, and another rumor of swimmers trying to mine the waters. Nothing came of either rumor.

Korean stevedores, considered the best in the world, clambered aboard, the hatch covers were drawn back and soon we heard the groan and "whump-whump" of the winches as the holds coughed up the last of their cargo of death.

Da Nang. Boats of a dozen descriptions suckling a floating dock, a cursory frisking by a South Vietnamese guard looking for American currency (you forgot the socks, man), then barbed wire, armored cars, and more barbed wire. There was a palm-lined street lined with buildings that showed the strong influence of the French colonial masters.

I stopped at a bar for a beer, called "33," and very good, and had a Vietnamese boy shine my shoes. He wanted 40 piasters (35 cents), pretty good money for a shoe shine in those days.

I had been foolishly calling the Vietnamese "Charlie," not realizing that that was the nickname given to the enemy Vietcong. I switched to "Jim." They didn't seem to mind being called "Charlie," though. I wonder if I had encountered some Vietcong.

I had a few beers with a group of South Vietnamese officers. They told me that the Vietcong were up in the hills and that they had killed many. This may have been an idle boast. I don't know.

As night fell a curfew went into effect. Da Nang recently had been under a twenty-four-hour curfew, but now the curfew ran from 8 P.M. to sunrise. I stayed at the Dong Khanh Hotel at 16 Dong Khanh St. It was run by a friendly old man with a crippled left arm who couldn't speak English.

Rule Number 2 at the Dong Khanh warns guests: "We are not responsible for every lost, so will you check for receipt your big money, camera, radio etc. in our office."

The Dong Khanh was overrun with little lizards—at least they looked like lizards. They zoomed around the floors, walls and ceilings and you would step on one and feel that awful squinchy feeling. And fleas. Fleas that bit in the night. A day later I was covered with dime-sized and quarter-sized red marks.

I stood on the balcony overlooking the street and could see flares fired at regular intervals from about 500 yards away. I gathered that they were lighting up some military installation to prevent the enemy from sneaking in. When I returned to the ship the next day the steward was waiting for me. "After breakfast, you come with me and we're going to see the old man," he said.

I had taken the day off without permission, and was to be logged—fined a day's pay and entered into the ship's log—for that offense, although my partner knew I was gone.

As I stood there, flanked by the steward, the captain read the charge: "Failure and neglect to perform his duties by being absent from his duties without permission." I was docked a day's pay ($10.09).

When the captain asked me if I had any remarks I replied, "None. . . . Well, all I can say is this, I don't have any." Not a very eloquent defense, but it beats "Homma-homma-homma-homma."

I'm glad I didn't say anything. I returned to my duties and gave my work a little extra. Three days later the charges were stricken from the log and I do believe I got my $10.09 back.

We left Da Nang on Jan. 4. Where to? No one knew. Some said Korea, Hawaii, Hong Kong.

Our first stop was determined by a crewman who fell to the deck and injured his back. We dropped him off in Subic Bay. Then we headed north around Luzon and then south to pick a course line for—it was finally posted in the crew's mess—the Panama Canal.

The ship, now in ballast, was not making good time and was not taking the seas well. On rough days she would leap a wave and come crashing down with a shudder that made it feel she would break in two. These shudders were almost always followed by a reduction in speed, and one day I heard the third mate say, "Well, one of these days we might exceed ten knots." But then the monsoon winds came from astern, and we made good time.

There were problems with the evaporator, which was not producing enough water for engines and crew. We were to stop in Honolulu to fill the tanks. Honolulu!

I pondered my situation, for Australia was to be my next stop. I paid a visit to the captain. I told him that if I could get off in Honolulu it would save me $400 and two weeks' travel time getting to Australia. Would he let me sign off in Honolulu? He would not.

Later I saw him talking to the steward, and the steward later said the captain had told him to bring my pay records up to date because he figured I was going to jump ship. There was a problem: I had 100 pounds of luggage aboard, in four bags. Usually, if a seaman jumps ship he merely grabs his seabag and runs for it. I needed porters.

We docked in Honolulu on Saturday, January 25. I jumped ship right after the noon meal. My porters consisted of one of the other mess boys and a recent friend, the boxer who had vowed to kill me in Subic Bay.

I returned to the dock area a day later. The *Tucson Victory* was gone. She had put to sea at 0700 Sunday. I shouldn't have been surprised that she got under way thirteen hours late.

I visited the offices of the ship's agent in Honolulu. The captain had wired my pay there. After deductions for supplies and cigarettes it came to $545 on gross pay of $1,139. I stayed at a very pleasant YMCA in Honolulu where I wrote much of this story. Then I gave my portable typewriter to the ship's agent.

I had wanted to make this trip around the world a strictly surface thing. I tried to find a job on a ship heading for Australia, or close to it, but was not successful. Finally, I arranged to fly on BOAC (British Overseas Airway Corporation, now British Airways) to Australia via Fiji and New Zealand.

5

Australia

I flew to Nandi, Fiji for a one-day stopover, then on to Auckland, New Zealand. I ran into an engineer from Los Angeles and we rented a car and drove to Wellington.

We stopped at various tourist attractions along the way—caves (of which there are plenty), wild rivers, thermal springs, lakes. It is all this geological activity—the constant quaking and steaming combined with isolation—that makes New Zealand a tough place to live for some, and the country has a high suicide rate. But it is one of the most beautiful places on earth. The people—whom the Australians call Kiwis—were extraordinarily friendly and helpful. It appeared they hadn't seen many Americans.

New Zealanders like to dress in white garments and indulge in lawn bowling. And they love gardening. Everywhere we went we saw beautifully landscaped and magnificently coiffeured gardens, the prettiest I have ever seen. It is the beauty of the gardens that is my lasting memory of this island nation.

On Sunday I took a train back to Wellington, then flew to Sydney and took a train to Melbourne.

My first impression of Australia: It is a country with a British mother and an absentee American father. American influence was everywhere—IBM, Xerox, General Motors-Holden, Pan Am, Safeway stores, Kentucky Fried Chicken, Woolworth's. The Australians resented this foreign influence and wanted desperately to be independent of it, but were not powerful enough to do that. The crown—represented by Queen Elizabeth II—held enormous power over the Commonwealth, and the queen could, if she wished, yank an elected prime minister from office. She did just that to Australia in the 1970s.

Australia's dependence upon, and servile attitude toward, the United States was the stuff of cartoons. One showed an Australian handing the newly inaugurated American President Richard Nixon a leash, at the end of which was a dog named Australia. The caption: "Here, he goes with the job."

Once in Melbourne, I got a room at an inexpensive hotel, the Cecil. Soon enough I was in a place called the Phoenix, the pub where the *Herald* staffers hung out. And there they were: The editor, Stu Brown, who told me he liked Americans, but not America, and thought the U.S. was a big bully. He said that during World War II he would row out into the harbor to visit American warships so he could beg a cup of decent coffee. He wanted to visit the United States, but couldn't get a visa because of his leftist leanings.

There was sub-editor (copy editor) Bob Millington, who could recite the Pledge of Allegiance, and always ended it " . . . with liberty and justice for all—except Negroes, Indians, pinkos . . . "

There was senior editor Geoff Clancy, who, as a police reporter, aided in the capture of an escaped prisoner. Clancy, who was on the scene to report the story, ended up joining the manhunt in a wooded area for the "bloody crim," as such creatures are sometimes called. He stumbled upon the escapee and called out. The escapee approached Clancy and surrendered, saying he'd rather give up to a journalist than the dreaded police. Clancy walked the escapee to a police car.

There was Peter Coster (PEEtah KOSStuh), the office cutup, who was like a cross between Kelsey Grammer and Charles Laughton (if you can imagine it.) Coster once approached me and, with his hands clasped behind his back and rocking back and forth proudly, said, "I've had three Yankee bee-ahs. Budweezer, Miller's and Schultz." I told him I would allow the Budweezer, but was he sure that Schultz was not supposed to be Schlitz? Coster started to giggle, his jowls resembling a pair of crimson apples.

There was movie-star handsome John Larkins, recently returned from London, where he had worked on the West Hem (Western Hemisphere) desk at Reuters News Service on Fleet Street. John offered to supply me with a letter of introduction to Reuters. I gratefully accepted the offer, and I used it.

A day later I met my primary boss, John Fitzgerald, the chief of staff (metro editor.) He told me that when the *Herald* heard that President Kennedy was shot in Dallas on November 22, 1963, the staff broke out its maps of Dallas, determined where the shooting occurred, got on the phone and called the hospital closest to the site. They got Parkland Memorial Hospital and were connected to an orderly in the emergency room just as the fatally wounded president was being wheeled in. They got an interview that they sold over a wide area.

The *Herald* was constantly "on the horn," calling all over the world. Australia subscribes to the same world that we do—roughly an axis formed by New York, London, Paris, Bonn (now Berlin), Rome and Washington. So in order to connect with it, they get on the phone—quite often. I wondered what the *Herald*'s phone bill looked like.

The *Herald* staff contained a number of recent arriv-als from the British Isles. These people were called pom-mies, after "prisoner of Mother England," dating to the days when Australia was a penal colony. A pommy who found it difficult to adjust to life in Australia and com-plained about it a lot was called a "pommy whinger" (WINN-jah), as in "Oh, 'e's just a bloody pommy whinger." I once cornered a pair of pommies who were trying desperately not to whinge. They complained qui-etly that all the Australians seemed to think about was "Beer, birds (girls) and footy (football)."

The *Herald* staffers accused me of speaking with a "Yankee drawl," which I thought was a contradiction in terms. And I would say, "Come on, you people, I don't drawl." And they would say "There! He did it again!"

Since my last place of employment was Chicago, I was sometimes called "Chicago Steve." One day someone brought a viola case into the news room. Geoff Clancy laughingly attributed ownership to me. He figured there was a tommy gun in the case and I had brought it along to wipe out members of the Bugs Moran gang or something.

Australians have their own peculiar manner with the English language, speaking something called Strine (for Australian). Strine leaves out consonants and concen-trates on vowels. For instance, we Americans pronounce smoke "smoke," as in oak. The Aussies (I perhaps should say some of them) pronounce that word "smaeiouke." An Australian—or an American—can affect the clipped Oxford accent. And Australians can speak American. But I have never heard an American successfully imitate an Aussie accent. It's not the words; it's those vowels!

In Strine, the dictionary is arranged in afferbet lau-der, and a device used to cool a room is called an egg-nishner.

The Australians have borrowed a lot of their social customs from England. So if you are invited to "tea," bring your appetite, because tea means dinner. And I distinctly heard this in an Australian home: "Ay, Mabel, the dawg 'asn't 'ad its tea yet." Then there's fair dinkum. It means genuine, as in "Carleton beat South Melbourne 186–110—fair dinkum!" The term also finds its way into newspaper headlines.

The Australians—like the English—have different names for a car's parts. The windshield is the windscreen, the hood is the bonnet, the car is fueled with petrol and the trunk is the boot. If someone honks at you for your poor driving habits you stick your head out the window and yell "In yer boot!"

There is "Have a good A" and "thirdeen." But, as in England, when you die they take you to a semmett tree.

One has to be careful with the Australian vocabulary. The words "root" and "probe" have vulgar connotations. A "napkin" is a diaper, and our napkin is called a "serviette."

Different spellings, too. Jail is "gaol" and curb is "kerb." What we call a "guy" they call a "bloke," and that term was commonly used.

There were a lot of other differences one had to get used to. A pharmacist was a chemist, an auto body repairman was a panel beater, a fruit merchant was a fruiterer or fruitologist. And some of their businesses had charming names, like the Four and Twenty Blackbird pie company and Great Caesar's Ghost motel.

The *Herald* had a sort of supra news editor with the title Copy Taster. It was like ordering frozen custard at Kopp's. You presented your story at the order window, then went to the pickup window further down the line to retrieve it. If it didn't show up, well, too bad. Your magnum opus would end up in a landfill near Geelong or somewhere. If the Copy Taster liked your story, you would be promptly notified and it would go through the editing process and make the paper. Alas, too many of my endeavors ended up in that Geelong landfill.

The *Herald* was an afternoon paper of 503,000 circulation that shared presses with its sister, the morning tabloid, the *Sun*, circulation 649,000. The *Herald* had the best writing of any paper I ever was associated with. One reason was the great number of writers of Irish descent. In the book "Madhouse on Madison Street," the author said the best writers were Irish and Jewish. I agree with that, although I'm neither Irish nor Jewish—not for 2,000 years anyway. But another reason I thought the *Herald* writers were outstanding was that they all could take shorthand and could fill their stories with wonderful (and accurate) quotes.

In Australia, journalism is considered a trade, not a profession. Its journalists are not college-educated. The country has a six-five-one school system, compared with America's six primary, six secondary. In Australia, after completing the equivalent of junior year in high school, people venture into the trades, journalism among them. If the student wants to go to college, he takes the 12th year of schooling, called matriculation, or college prep. But only about 8 percent of Australians go on to college, compared with more than 40 percent in the United States. Newspapers like the *Herald* were hiring journalists at what was the equivalent of the end of their junior year in high school, so the youngest were only seventeen, in a few cases even sixteen. These journalists then embarked on a four-year cadetship, at the end of which they would be required to take 100 words per minute of Pitman shorthand. They then were graded, D, C, B, A and A-plus. The

Herald accorded me the grade A, which I certainly didn't deserve under their standards and which caused some problems with the other staffers, a majority of whom were graded C.

The idea of shorthand has long intrigued me. I regret never learning it. When I worked for the *Sheboygan Press* there was a reporter named Al Nagy, graduate of Ohio State, who studied shorthand (Gregg) on his own and said it was more valuable to him than anything he learned in journalism school. As I look back on my own journalism education, I find there were few courses that stand out as valuable. Law of the Press (which should be expanded) was one and Photography another. If I were entering college to study journalism today, the first course I would sign up for would be shorthand. I also wish journalism schools had a course called "Bias." I did my first professional work as a journalist before I had any formal training in the field. If I compare the pre- and post-education stories I do not notice a difference. Frankly, I think journalism schools graduate too many people who simply cannot write.

Regularly you will encounter stories in the American press where three different reporters covering the very same press conference will come away with three different quotes. Reporters nowadays use tape recorders, but I think shorthand would be much more valuable and efficient. And shorthand does not require batteries. The Australian journalists used shorthand not just to capture quotes, but for general note-taking. Very efficient. I was truly impressed by the Australian system.

During their cadetships, the journalism students are periodically tested on current events and their scores would be posted on the staff bulletin board. Such a cadetship progam had another advantage. It added a youthful dimension to journalism. Indeed, the *Herald* featured a column, "Under 20," written and edited by teenage staffers.

Australia, like America at the time, paid women considerably less than men for the same work. In fact, it was common to see classified ads in which a job was offered and its description was followed by "women paid 50 percent less." I thought it would be great to open a business in Australia and hire only women. Save 50 percent on your payroll. But that probably wouldn't be allowed. Australian women were gorgeous. And these were the days of the miniskirt, including the micro-mini. Wow! The old cardiovascular harness was thumpin' away like a bass solo by Slam Stewart.

The female staffers at the *Herald* would cluster in self-protective little groups in corners of the pub while the men would belly up to the bar. This seemed to be the accepted way of doing things. Women were treated like second-class citizens, from pay through social status.

The *Herald*—like Australia in general—took a cavalier view of the world to which it subscribed but did not live in. While I was there the *Herald* ran a story on page one about a rebellious governor of a Caribbean island, St. Kitts, I believe. The governor wanted to pull his island out of a three-island federation and become independent. The crown (British government) said no, these islands must remain a part of the federation. The governor was defiant, and the crown vowed action.

In an American paper this story likely would rate the hed "Britain vows to crush mini-revolt," or "Rebel governor faces British wrath"—something like that. The *Herald* ran a picture on page one of the governor gazing into the sky for the plane bearing the British troops who would enforce the crown's edict. The hed: "The British are coming, ta-rah, ta-rah!"

Such irreverence was common. I once did a story about the problem of alcoholism in the state of Victoria, a problem there as elsewhere. I interviewed a recovering alcoholic, who spun a tale of the woes of alcohol addiction. I wrung every Dickensian tear I could from the story. Her addiction caused her to lose her job, she said. Then her husband left her, and her family turned against her (violins, please). She sank into the Hades of alcoholism (a little "Francesca da Rimini" might be appropriate here) and hit bottom. Then she pulled herself together, swore off drink and began to rebuild her life (definitely some Beethoven here). And so I wrote the story. It survived the copy taster's scrutiny and made its way into the paper. The day it appeared I flipped through the *Herald* to see what kind of treatment my masterpiece got. The hed: "Mother is a drunk." An overline noted the number of cases of alcoholism in Victoria. To this day I hope the woman didn't read that and become so depressed she went back on the bottle again.

The *Herald* wanted to send me on a driving trip around the state of Victoria. But first I had to acquire a Victorian driver's license. Australians drive on the left, of course. I wasn't so daunted by this, but I failed the written test. Among the questions I missed was when a driver should yield right-of-way to a tram. How stupid of me! The answer, of course, is "always." I passed the test second time around and got through the driving part with no difficulty. I ended up driving more than 1,000 miles on the left without incident. The only habit I never broke was that I would always enter the car from the left side, then sit there, like a dummy, looking for the steering wheel. Which reminds me of a joke: Arnie and Stosh,

Siamese twins joined at the hip, lived on the south side of Milwaukee. A reporter for the *Milwaukee Journal Sentinel* interviewed them. He asked Arnie, the twin on the left, "How do you guys get along?" And Arnie says, "Oh, we get along just fine. But we're movin' to Australia next month." The reporter asks, "What for?" And Arnie says, "I want Stosh to do the drivin' for a change."

For some reason or other, Australians, while driving on the left, must yield to the right. And Australian drivers had a terrifying habit of rushing up to a stop sign and slamming on the brakes at the last second. On too many occasions they didn't stop in time, which made Australia a world leader in what they called "T-bone crashes." I once told Peter Coster that I thought the Australian drivers were the worst in the world. "They're worse in INjah," he said. Well, I vowed never to visit that place.

With Aussie driver's license in wallet, I began my long trip around Victoria. Some staffers figured that as long as I would be traveling through the wine country I might bring back a few flagons of Australia's finest. Australia produces excellent wines. I was particularly fond of a drop called Coonawarra claret. On this trip I saw kangaroos in the wild for the first time in my life. There were three of 'em, between Boggy Creek and Jim and Jack's Creek. They were sitting in the middle of the road as I approached, and they bounded off in three directions, scaring the daylights out of me. Kangaroos—called roos in headlines, or kangas if the hed writer has more room—are as common in Victoria as are deer in Wisconsin. The difference is that kangaroos can jump—leaps of more than thirty feet have been documented. And they can grow to be fairly large—200 pounds, perhaps more, for a big red. One *Herald* staffer told me of a driver who was tooling down a bush road in his Volkswagen Beetle when he heard a very loud "whump." He looked up to see the roof of his car caved in. A leaping kangaroo had landed squarely atop his car.

About three-fourths of Australia is arid to semi-arid. Mountains ring the coasts, and most people live there, in pleasant and moist enough climates. The most spectacular thing I saw on my trip was Wilson's Promontory, a huge, rocky outcropping on the Victorian coast. Awesome.

On the other side of the coastal range is the outback, flat, barren, boring. Australia is a geologically mature country, so the river beds are shallow, and during spring and fall rains the rivers overflow, causing flooding that blocks roads and prevents traffic from getting through. That means the lorries cannot supply the outback pubs with beer, a cause of great consternation in this beer-loving nation. When I was there the pub in Birdsville, New South Wales, north of Melbourne, ran out of beer during the flooding. This page one story was turned over to an old veteran, Doug (Stainless) Steele (who also helped me fill out my Australian tax forms). Slim Dusty, Australia's Johnny Cash, sang a sad song, "The Pub With No Beer," about this spring and fall happening. The lyrics, as I recall them:

Ohhhhh, it's lonesome awaaaaaay
From your kindred and all.
By the campfire at night
Where the wild dingoes caw-all
But it's nowhere as lonely
Or morbid or drear
Than to stand at the bar
Of the pub with no beer.
Old Billy the Blacksmith

First time in his life
Came home cold sober
To his darlin' wife.
And when the missus asked him
"What ARE you doing here?"
He broke down and told her
"The pub's out of beer."

The *Herald* at this time did not have a Sunday paper. So on nothing-ever-happens-on-Saturdays the deputy chief of staff would sit in the news room alone while a skeleton crew of staffers would hang out at the Phoenix pub. If the COS needed a journalist to cover anything he would simply get on the horn and call the pub and ask for one. One day a story did pop up. Someone won $10,000 or so in the Tattersall's lottery. The COS called the Phoenix. Peter Coster answered. The COS told Coster about the story and asked that a journalist be sent over. Coster said "Wait a minute!" Pretty soon Coster was back on the line. He said, "Nope, nobody wants to cover it," and hung up. I wondered what would have happened if Raging Bull Wills had been the COS that day. It was this sense of playfulness that endeared me to the Australians.

I had difficulty finding inexpensive lodgings since I was to be in Melbourne only a few months. I got a batch of listings from the paper and one day hired a cab to find a place. I ended up in what they call a "bed-sitting room" on Washington Street in the "excloosif" suburb of Toorak. That was not smart. It would be comparable to a journalist from Melbourne getting a job at the *Milwaukee Journal Sentinel* and renting a place on Canberra St. in Elm Grove. I should have taken digs in the rough neighborhood of Fitzroy. But I loved my little place.

I also found out that there was such a thing as a Toorak accent. Certain words were pronounced differently. It was like the difference between Milwaukee's south side and north side. Also, after a while, the American accent sounds strange, even to an American. I encountered a few Americans in my stay there, and I must agree, if Americans don't sound strange, they certainly sound distinctive.

Herald staffers told me of an uppity sort from one of the wealthier suburbs—perhaps Toorak or South Yarra—who was running for parliament. He was being interviewed over a local radio station. The interviewer asked: "Some people seem to think you are a snob. Would you care to comment on that?" The candidate says, "Snob? If I were a snob, why would I be appearing on a low-class show like this?"

The Melbourne phone system had a nasty habit of going down after rainstorms. And the dial tone sounded like someone gargling.

Australia's immigration patterns were identical to those of the U.S.: Potato Famine Irish, Germans fleeing conscription, Lutherans feeling Catholics, Catholics fleeing Lutherans, Jews fleeing everyone, Poles, Russians. No blacks. Australia, while quite tolerant inwardly, did not accept black immigrants. At the time I was there the three main immigrant groups were Italians, Hungarians and Greeks. There were occasional stories complaining that these people were clinging to their language and culture and refusing to become Australianized.

Victoria was very heavily Irish and there were times I felt like I was in Ireland. Andy Capp types abounded. If you're looking for the quintessential Aussie, Paul "Crocodile Dundee" Hogan will suffice nicely, although he is from Sydney. A onetime bridge painter, Hogan complained to a Sydney TV station that what they passed off as humor wasn't funny at all. The station wrote Hogan that, well, if you think you're so funny, why don't you come over and show us what you've got. It led to Hogan getting a TV show. One of his more hilarious skits was a contest, "Dinner With Hogan." He invited people to submit their names. Apparently thousands of people wanted to have dinner with this guy, because at contest's end he had a huge drum full of names. Hogan turned the drum, then opened it, reached in and pulled out the lucky winner. It was Queen Elizabeth II! So Hogan explained to the queen which bus to take to his house, where to transfer and so on.

Football was the subject of constant debate with the *Herald* staffers. They referred to American football as "gridiron." Because gridiron players wore so much protective gear, the Aussies thought it was a soft sport compared to Australian Rules Football, in which unprotected players slammed into each other at full speed and suffered all sorts of fractures, bruises and cuts. And their game was truly magnificent. To get the peon's feel for the game, you would get a ticket to stand in "the outer," then scrounge up a pair of empty pint beer cans, stand on them to get a better view and hobble around and shout such Australian things as "Good on yer, Fitzie!" I was very impressed by the accuracy of the kickers. They could boot the ball long distances on the straightaway or, more impressively, they could boot it at angles with uncanny accuracy. American professional teams should go down there and look for punters.

The ball is larger than the American football, and is rounded at the ends rather than pointed. (After my trip, in a speech to a group of fifth graders at St. Peter Claver

School in Sheboygan, I described the ball as looking like a small brown watermelon. The teacher had the children write up reports on my talk and showed them to me. One boy had written: "In Australia they play a real funny game. They kick a small brown watermelon around.")

One defender of American football was Lou, owner of the Phoenix pub and a former Australian Rules Football player. He had seen Super Bowl III, in which the New York Jets beat the heavily favored Baltimore Colts. Lou lined up three bar stools, crouched behind them, and barked out some nonsensical commands in his imitation of quarterback Joe Namath. Then he rushed forward, knocking the bar stools over. It was hilarious.

The Aussies were fascinated by the American passing game. Wisely, I brought an American football along, and one day I showed a few Aussies how to grasp it and toss it. Within minutes they were throwing perfect spirals twenty yards and more.

One day I was interviewing a psychologist at one of the universities for a story about something or other. He detected my accent and asked, "What part of the States are you from?" I said, "Wisconsin." He said, "Oh, the Green Bay Packers!" A year earlier, he was in Atlanta and a friend of his took him to the Atlanta Falcons–Green Bay Packers game. The Packers won 38–7. He was most impressed.

Working as a journalist in Australia was quite different from America. Australia does not have a U.S.-style Constitution, and no Bill of Rights with its First Amendment. While working on the police beat I found that there was a most complicated law that states you cannot mention the name of the accused in the same sentence that you describe the crime that was committed. Also, once a person is accused of a crime the press is not allowed to comment on the issue until the case comes to trial. Rules governing the press are very strict. And then there's something called the Secrets Act. Don't even ask.

Australia struck me as what the United States would have been had the colonists not decided to revolt against King George III. The queen is the mom, all right. I once covered a meeting of the Wool Board. (Australia has boards for everything. There was a Grain Board, an Egg Board, a Milk Board. There probably was even a Board Board.) Before addressing the Wool Board, the speaker raised a glass of wine and said, "To the queen." And all those present raised their glasses of wine and mumbled, "To the queen." Except me. I suddenly felt like a 1770s American colonist. I just could not bring myself to drink to the queen. I felt this was exactly what would be happening in America if it hadn't broken with the crown. It was one of the strangest feelings I had in my life. (However, I did later drink the wine.)

Editor Stu Brown let me extend my stay with the paper until September. In the meantime I met an Australian lovely named Margaret, a nurse (they call nurses "sisters"). She looked just like Anne Morrow Lindbergh. A doll. We embarked on a wonderful romance. We would rendezvous at the Southern Cross Hotel (not what you're thinking), visit the wine shop there and pick up a bottle of Coonawarra claret, then head to our favorite bistro, Santisi's. Melbourne restaurants could not serve wine, but you could bring in your own bottle and for a modest "corkage fee" they would open the bottle and supply glasses. It was really neat.

Margaret's father was dying of Lou Gehrig's disease. Margaret's family would invite me over on Sundays, and on those days they would take their father for a ride through the Grampians, a mountain range outside Melbourne that the man dearly loved. By this time the father could not move his arms and legs, and the family developed a method in which they would put him in a blanket and literally pour him into the car. The tender and loving care they lavished on that man would bring tears to my eyes. He died less than a year later.

I was often invited to Margaret's house for "tea," after which we would join her brother, John, and his wife, Sue, in games of Scrabble and Monopoly, a game at which John was merciless.

Margaret's family was mirthful and delightful. I had totally fallen in love with Margaret, and they were all bemused by that. Her Uncle Harold said, "One Yank and they're off." Margaret and I did discuss marriage—quite seriously, in fact. But she didn't want to leave Australia, and while I liked the place I didn't know if I wanted to settle there. I gave that some thought. And one day I met an American woman who had married an Australian after World War II and settled in Australia. "Don't do it," she said. "The adjustment is too difficult." She had settled in Australia, but missed America terribly.

The *Chicago Daily News*, the last paper I worked for in the States, cabled me one day and said a family from Chicago had emigrated to Australia and now was living in a processing center for new arrivals outside of Brisbane. Could I fly up there and interview them? Certainly. Once in Brisbane, I bought two bottles of wine and sought out the family. I handed them the bottles of wine, and launched into the interview. I got the distinct impression that these people—parents with three teenage children—had left Chicago to escape the racial problems there. They were now in the process of obtaining Australian drivers' licenses and had made an offer on a home.

I never checked back to see if they remained in Australia. My guess is that they didn't.

I went to the *Brisbane Courier-Mail*, which was associated with the *Melbourne Herald*, and they let me use a typewriter to write the story. Then I arranged for the *Courier-Mail* to cable the story to Chicago. The paper never charged me for that cable! A *Courier-Mail* editor asked if he could use my story. He said the *Courier-Mail* had sent a reporter to interview the Chicago family, but the family refused to talk to him. He probably should have brought a couple bottles of wine!

*   *   *

A travel agent arranged the next leg of my trip. I would take a cargo-passenger vessel, the *Arafura*, to Japan. Then I would board a Russian ship, the *Baikal*, for the voyage to Nakhodka. From there I would take a seven-day rail journey across the then-Soviet Union to Moscow on the Trans-Siberian. I would be traveling what was called "second (hard) class." And I thought the Soviet Union was a classless society. This was the lowest class foreigners were allowed to travel.

I enjoyed a huge round of goodbyes with *Herald* staffers and other Australians I had met. John Fitzgerald, the chief of staff, took me to dinner. He said that if he had my experience he would stay in Australia and would set up a business catering to U.S. trade missions. He said he'd been thinking of doing such a thing himself.

I left Melbourne by train on Wednesday, September 3. Margaret saw me off at the Spencer Street train station. It was a sad farewell. I was in love. We were talking about getting married, and would discuss that later. Margaret was wearing the string of pearls I had given her the day

before. She had presented me with a gold ballpoint pen
and ordered me to use it often in writing her. As I kissed
her and hugged her goodbye, she said, ''I am not going to
cry.'' But I think she did.

I never saw her again.

6

Arafura

I stayed in Sydney for two days waiting for my ship, the *Arafura*, to leave. It was a cargo-passenger liner, so did not keep to a strict schedule. Saturday, Sept. 6, I boarded the *Arafura* in Sydney Harbor.

There was a telegram from Margaret. "Bon voyage. I love you." That wiped me out.

The *Arafura* was a beautiful fifteen-year old vessel with accommodations for twelve passengers. There were only two passengers this time, a Japanese fellow named Junji Suzuki and myself. Junji was the Japanese representative for the P&O (Peninsular and Oriental) shipping line. He was making out a report in English. I helped him edit and type it.

The ship was carrying a varied cargo to Yokkaichi, about 4,400 miles from Sydney, and would visit some other ports in Japan. The captain was fortyish, tall, slender, athletic, and about the last person on earth central casting would choose as a sea captain. He was a tennis enthusiast and history buff, which made him a delightful dining companion. He also played chess, and I beat him—and Junji as well. The captain had an electric organ in his cabin and was learning to play it.

Junji and I took our meals at the captain's table along with the chief engineer and other officers. The messman who served us looked like Mao Tse-tung.

I was curious about the economics of these cargo-passenger ships. The captain said that if they were carrying the full complement of twelve passengers their fares would pay the food bill for everyone on board. The twelve-passenger maximum was set because of insurance restrictions.

The captain said we were taking the very same course the Japanese "Tokyo Express" took during World War II. He said the *Arafura* had called on ports in China and the Soviet Union, including Nakhodka, where I was headed. On British charts Nakhodka is on American Bay.

Food was superb. Sometimes dessert was cheddar cheese. How British! Also, a steward would deliver tea and biscuits (cookies) to our cabins each morning at 10:30 and each afternoon at 3:30. I'm just not the tea and biscuits type and I finally got the steward to stop these deliveries.

It also was customary for the captain and other officers to invite us passengers to their cabins for drinks before dinner. And we passengers reciprocated.

The officers were very young. The chief (first) mate was only twenty-five, the second mate twenty-three, and the two third mates were twenty-two. One of those, Andre Bezkorovainy, whose family emigrated to Australia from Russia, also was the cargo officer. Since I was going to be traveling on the Trans-Siberian, I was curious about Russia. He said he had two brothers still living there. Andre later visited me in Wisconsin and got his first taste of snow. We still exchange Christmas cards.

In the afternoons we would play deck golf. Occasionally in the evening there would be open-air dinner parties on deck.

The captain said that when the *Arafua* reached age twenty she would be torn up for scrap because marine underwriters would not insure "bottoms" (as Lloyds of London calls vessels) that are more than twenty years old.

It is sad to think that such a beautiful ship would end up in the scrap yard.

We crossed the equator on September 11. We arrived in Yokkaichi at 4 P.M. on September 18 and unloaded some cargo there. The captain allowed me to stay aboard for two more stops, Nagoya and Kobe, where I finally left the vessel on September 21.

The *Arafura*'s radioman and another crewman introduced me to a delightful restaurant in Kobe that served a dish called yakatori. It amounts to pieces of meat—chicken, pork, shrimp, or fish on a skewer, and roasted over a charcoal fire. This is served with a bowl of rice and a bowl of mild soy sauce for dipping. Sake (rice wine) is optional. It was one of the most delicious dishes I have had in my life. One day, at Murasaki's yakatori parlor in Nagoya, I had fifteen sticks of yakatori, plus the rice and saki.

At the Motomachi shopping center I checked out the stamps for sale. One stamp, from Mongolia, commemorated the American astronauts' first-ever landing on the moon in July. The stamp showed the astronauts on the moon stumbling across a Soviet space capsule.

Japan was expensive. Even in that year, 1969, a good steak dinner could set you back $40. Lodgings were expensive. In Kobe I first stayed at the YMCA, then the Flying Angel hotel, recommended by officers on the *Arafura*. I also stayed at youth hostels. One cost only $1.25 a night.

American influence abounds in Japan, from "basebaru" to "hot dodogus" to "bye, bye," which I heard the Japanese use often. The Japanese were friendly and about a third of them spoke some English.

I arranged to get train tickets to Hiroshima. The Japanese "bullet trains" whiz people from city to city at well over 100 miles an hour. They are truly marvelous. My train carried me through Akaski, Kakogawa, Gochaku, Himeji, Tatsumo, Wake, Okayama, Kurashiki, Fukuyama, Akasaka, Matsunaga, Onomichi, Itozaki, Mihara and Sayo. As we whizzed from city to city, I could make out Mount Fuji in the distance. It was a beautiful country.

I bought a box lunch, served in a thin wooden container. Inside was a work of art. There were three neat rows of white rice with floral decorations on them in black rice. There was a pile of black pasta-looking stuff that on closer inspection proved to be teensy-weensy fish, like guppies. There was a piece of seaweed, a piece of what seemed to be kohlrabi and another vegetable that I couldn't recognize. I got tea in a little plastic throwaway pot. All this was delicious.

I was enthralled by the young mother in the seat in front of me. Using chopsticks, she was feeding her two small children like a mother bird feeding her young. The mother's chopsticks were a perfect extension of her thumb and forefinger, and I don't believe she could have performed her feeding chores any more efficiently if she merely used her fingers. Her dexterity with those chopsticks was amazing.

The Peace Park in Hiroshima, located on the spot where the atomic bomb fell in August 1945, is truly a depressing place. The museum there contains grisly artifacts from the attack, including displays of fingernails and shredded clothing and photos of injured and incinerated bomb victims.

One display showed leaflets that American planes had dropped, warning that a terrible bomb was coming their way. But the Japanese felt the United States didn't give them ample warning, and the message conveyed was that this brutal monster called the United States was bullying poor Japan. I thought, who started this war? What about the Rape of Nanking? What about Pearl Harbor?

I also visited the ancient temples at Miajima Fuji and took in the usual tourist sites. It was truly impressive and picturesque country. And clean. At the railroad stations, between trains, a white-gloved attendant would walk the tracks and, with a pair of tongs, pick up debris and put it in a container. Then he would hurl a bucket of water on the train platform and run a broom across it. As a train came through the station the attendant would face it and salute. Then he would turn toward the train as it passed through, then turn again, holding his salute until the train cleared the station. Marvelous! Amtrak should do that!

I arrived in Yokohama on September 25, got a room and then ventured down to the dockyard to check out the *Baikal*, the Russian ship I would be taking the next day to Nakhodka. It was docked at the South Pier. I can't describe the strange feeling that came over me as I saw the *Baikal*. It was painted white, had a single yellow stack with a red band around it and a golden sickle and hammer on that. The *Baikal* was to be my home for two days on a trip that would take me across the entire Soviet Union. This was in the days of the Cold War, when U.S.-Soviet relations were not the best.

I boarded the *Baikal* at 9 A.M. on Saturday, September 27. Customs inspection was remarkably swift, and all the people were pleasant. Once aboard I was surprised to find that most of the crew could handle the English language very well. And they were truly friendly.

In the bar I ran into Tom, a U.S. merchant marine officer who had been born in Scotland, and Hans Herman Henschel from West Germany, who told us he had been named for two uncles killed during World War II.

At departure time the passengers flocked to the deck. A small Russian band was playing something that sounded like rock music, people waved, streamers were hurled, the ship's whistle blew and we edged away from the dock as people below waved and cheered. It was quite a sendoff, one that I never expected. I thought the Russians were supposed to be dour, humorless people. They were precisely the opposite.

The Russians mix the sexes in public transportation. When I got to my cabin, No. 232, I found I had been placed with two Hungarian men and an attractive Finnish blonde. But when the blonde saw this deal she went to the purser's office to arrange something different. One of the Hungarians also moved, so there was just one Hungarian and myself in the cabin, which was quite comfortable, even though it did not have a private bath, merely a sink. A number of cabins had to share a bathroom in the passageway.

Lunch in the dining room was delicious. A big sardine (I think it was a sardine), small sliced tomatoes and cucumbers, a seasoned hamburger patty with french-fried onions, rice with pimentos, and for dessert, coffee with a scoop of ice cream in it. I found the food throughout the voyage to be tasty but a tad monotonous.

The passengers were mainly Japanese, with a sprinkling of Russians, Hungarians, Germans, Finns, Koreans, Swiss, Canadians, Bulgarians, Czechs, British, and French. There were two elderly couples from Altoona, Pennsylvania, and a Navy doctor named James Stewart, recently discharged after serving in Vietnam. He told me he had wanted to take the Trans-Siberian home after his discharge, but that the brass opposed it. Finally his superiors relented, but told him "Find an American traveling companion." And Stewart said to me, "You're my traveling companion." We would have a ball.

We encountered a Hungarian woman named Maria, who worked in the East German embassy in Budapest.

She had the most fascinating green eyes I have ever seen. She focused her greenies on Tom, the sea officer, but he cooled when he found out she was married. Maria enlisted me as her envoy to deal with Tom. She handed me a note to give to him. The message, written in English, was not sealed. And I, being a very very nasty person, read it before delivering it. It was well written. I never told anyone about this until now, thirty-four years later, and so I share it with you: "Tom, I must tell you the truth, the man was my husband but I left him on the second day of our group. I can't tell you this story by English but I left him forever. You must come to Hungary, because you promised me believe me I left him forever, but this I don't want to tell you I shall waiting for you, don't be angry with me please, on the whole afternoon I was looking for you."

It didn't work. Tom would have nothing to do with the gorgeous Maria. But Hans Herman Henschel had no scruples about her being married, and he began pitching woo at the beauty. One day Tom and I were walking the deck and we came across Maria and Hans Herman sitting together on deck chairs. Rather than get upset, Tom walked over and launched into a song from *West Side Story*: "Maria . . . I just found a girl named Maria." Then he laughed and walked away. Hans Herman was furious.

I saw Maria a few days later. She wore green mascara and was dressed in a green kimono, complementing her fabulous green eyes. She gave me some phone numbers and told me to call her if I ever got to Budapest. I wondered what Maria was up to. I think she was a spy!

Down in the *Baikal* bar, our international group gathered to drink and get into conversations about world events. Tom and I would pick on Hans Herman, chiding him about Germany's role in World War II, the atrocities and the concentration camps and all. And Hans Herman, acting like a Milwaukee County supervisor, would say: "Ve didn't know vodt vas going on, and if ve did, vodt could ve do about idt?" Then he would walk over to the jukebox, pull out a few kopeks and play "Hava Nagela." I kid you not!

On the deck near the stern of the *Baikal* a large game board was painted where you could play chess with pieces that were about two feet tall. The chess pieces kept blowing over in the wind, making it difficult to keep track of the game. But we managed to get in a few.

The *Baikal* was a fairly new and rather attractive vessel perhaps 400 feet long. We were allowed to take tours of the ship, including the engine room (it was a diesel). On the bridge, the second mate showed me the teletype machine over which the *Baikal* got weather reports and other navigational information. All this stuff was in English. The second mate explained that English was the international language of travel and commerce, so all the sea officers knew how to read English.

The food continued to be excellent. For evening dinner we had frankfurters with mashed potatoes and pumpernickel-style bread. For some reason, butter (*maslo*) was served only with breakfast. And breakfast usually consisted of pieces of salami, an omelet, that wonderful pumpernickel bread with *maslo* and tea (*chai*).

The Russians continued to be pleasant, and the fellow travelers were entertaining to say the least. It was like taking part in a Broadway comedy.

7

Trans-Siberian

We arrived in Nakhodka, a very handsome seaport on American Bay, on Monday, September 29. Customs and immigration proceeded swiftly, but we were not allowed to carry our baggage ashore.

There was a duty-free shop where we could get vodka for $1.80 a liter and cigarettes—Camel filters—for sixteen cents a pack. The clerk wanted only American money.

We soon boarded our train. The rail cars, made in East Germany, were modern and comfortable. I was assigned a four-berth compartment with two funny Canadians and a humorless German named Herbert. Tom the sea officer and James Stewart, the Navy doctor, were in another part of the train, traveling in first class compartments that had two bunks. My second class arrangements were not bad at all. The berths, which doubled as seats, were upholstered and comfortable.

Moscow is 5,864 rail miles from Nakhodka. This was like boarding an eastbound train in Milwaukee and traveling by rail all the way to . . . to Moscow.

We arrived in Khabarovsk at 10:30 A.M. the next day. We transferred to another train, our baggage handled by porters who lugged them to the appropriate compartments. Tom and a few others decided to stay in Khabarovsk a few days. I was to encounter Tom six days later in Moscow. Jim Stewart and I remained on the train.

While in the Intourist Hall at the huge Khabarovsk station we were treated to an English-language program telling us about the Soviet contributions to peace. If one

75

listened carefully he would find that the word "Soviet" and the word "peace" were uttered close together. This would happen over and over until the listener began to associate the word "Soviet" with "peace." Very clever! The narrator had a New York accent. The Intourist Hall also had a ledger with the words "Your Impressions." I was impressed, and noted so. Other travelers obviously weren't. A young Intourist representative asked me what I thought of the way they were handling the trip and I said I thought they were doing quite well. "We get a lot of complaints," he said.

The next train was not nearly as modern or as clean as the Nakhodka to Khabarovsk train. Many of the windows in the doors between compartment were broken and many lights did not work. There was no hot water and no soap. We were pulled by a steam engine, and I don't believe we made more than thirty-five miles an hour. The people made up for the drabness.

The weather was getting nippy, much like our American November. We passed through magnificent birch and aspen forests and the trees were beginning to lose their leaves, covering the earth with a gold carpet that shimmered in the sunlight.

The Trans-Siberian at points runs as close as ten miles to the Chinese border. One day we passed a train pulling flatcars loaded with tanks. They probably were headed for the Ussuri region, which the USSR was contesting with China. There were, by Russian count, more than 500 border clashes with the Chinese since June of that year. Sometimes there were as many as fifty Russian officers and enlisted men on the train.

We were not supposed to take pictures of military things. The Intourist pamphlet, "Visit the USSR," which was printed in the United States, noted: "No restrictions apply to photography, and cine-photography in general, but you should avoid taking pictures of frontier stations, railway stations and military installations." I was a bad boy. I asked an Intourist official if I could take a picture of the train in the station. "Nyet!" he replied. Then I asked a porter if I could take a picture of the train in the station. "Da!" he said. So I took the picture.

Food continued to be delicious. For breakfast, diced ham and eggs were served in a mess kit with pumpernickel bread, butter and tea. The evening meal was steak with eggs and french fries, bread and tea. Sometimes we had borscht (beet soup).

Our dining car was served by a large, pleasant woman in her fifties who put in a fourteen-hour day. We dubbed her Mama. She hovered over us like a mother hen, shooing others away from our Intourist table. The dining car maitre d', if you want to call him that, was a bald man with thick glasses who looked like Telly Savalas. We nicknamed him Dr. No after the villain in the James Bond movie. He appeared to like that title.

Our compartment maid was a thirtyish, fun-loving woman named Amelia. She made sure everything was just so and enjoyed doing it. She was a delight.

There were some young Russian women on the train. They were as attractive as any you would find on America's college campuses. Sadly, as Russian women get older they tend to put on a lot of weight.

Russians love chess, and they are superb players. My most formidable opponent was a bearded intellectual who looked like a young Lenin. He got me in "SHAKH ma-tee" (check mate) so often that I dubbed him Vladimir Shakh.

The dining car and sleeping cars had several chess boards and Jim and I played lots of games with the Russians. They invariably killed us. I considered myself a decent player, but I played a finesse game, husbanding each piece. The Russians played smash-mouth chess. They just kept shoving players at you—ZOW-ZOW-ZOW. And when the smoke lifted from the carnage they would have one key player that you wouldn't have—perhaps a rook, a bishop or a knight. And they would give you that "gotcha" smile, because they now knew they were going to win that round. I do believe this was the way they beat the Germans in World War II. They just kept coming and coming until they had the advantage.

I did beat a Russian sea officer once. I caught him check mate in a knight trap—a move I learned from my brother Jim. He looked at the board, nodded, said something like "Ah—so!" and then slaughtered me in the rest of our games. I figured I was about three for fifty in chess games with the Russians. I could not compete with these people. Jim Stewart didn't have much luck against them either.

One day Stewart and I were enjoying a game of chess when a young Russian visited the dining car. His eyes opened wide and he gaped at us like we were animals in a zoo (not an uncommon experience for us on this trip). Then he ordered a bottle of wine and stood there and watched us drink it. Looking back on this, we should have got a third glass and had him join us. Ugly Americans!

I told Jim that many of these people were seeing Americans for the first time. The cold war was still on, so there was some friction between the United States and the Soviet Union, but it wasn't the fault of these people. Jim and I agreed that we should make sure they didn't think we were evil people, just regular Joes. We treated our Russian friends with courtesy and respect and they returned it.

One day a drunk accosted us between the train cars and began yelling and cursing. He yelled things like "*Amerikanski*," and "*journalista.*" I think he thought we were with the CIA or something. Amelia shooed him away. That was the only unpleasant encounter I had in my ten days in the Soviet Union.

One day Jim and I were playing chess and smoking Russian cigarettes, large, white, vile things with recessed filters. They looked like tampons. Dr. No came over and asked Jim, "You like Rosski cigarette? Iss goot?" Jim looked at Dr. No, smiled sweetly and said, "Mediocre. V-e-r-y mediocre." Dr. No accepted this as the highest compliment.

Another time, Jim and I sat down at our Intourist table and noticed a group of officers at a table farther down. They were drinking beer. We summoned Mama and motioned that we'd like some beer. She got very flustered. She went to the officers' table, then rushed past us to a compartment. She returned with two bottles of beer and presented them to us. We reached for rubles to pay for the beer. She shook her head and pointed at the officers. Hey! A Russian major gave me a bottle of beer from his private stock. We thanked him and he gave us a friendly wave.

The scenery throughout this trip was beautiful. There were vast forests of birch, beloved by the Russians and the theme of many stories and songs, and stands of pine, aspen, larch, spruce and fir. There were meadow steppes—large treeless plains—and wooded steppes, hillocky forest swamps, wooded bogs, lakes, hills, ridges, kettles and moraines. Two Canadians aboard said the scenery was exactly like that of Canada. In fact, Russia and Canada share much of the same latitude.

Most of the towns we passed through were little gatherings of cabins and shacks made of wooden slabs and mortar along streets of dirt and mud. For thousands of miles I did not see one paved road. There were very few cars and the most common mode of transport was the horse-drawn wagon.

As the train approached Irkutsk, three days west of Khabarovsk, Blondie, one of the women in charge of our car, woke us early so we could see the morning mists rise above lake Baikal, an enormous freshwater lake large enough to hold all the water in the Great Lakes.

The evening before, one of the Canadians helped Blondie build a fire in the coal stove that heated the car. Blondie was complaining of a headache. The Canadian gave her one of his headache pills. Instead of curing her headache, it made her nauseous and she threw up.

Most of the Westerners left the train in Irkutsk. Jim Stewart and I remained, and I'm almost certain that at this point we were the only two Americans aboard.

Irkutsk is home to the Irkutsk Institute of Technology. A group of Russians in their thirties, some from the institute, boarded the train here. I counted thirty-one of them. I had stepped onto the train platform for a smoke. As I returned to my compartment, I was shocked. Three Russian women, all about my age, were packing their belongings in the room. It dawned on me swiftly: The Russians mix the sexes in public transportation. Oh-oh. I volunteered to take an upper berth, then sought out Amelia. I found her at the end of the car. I gave her my most menacing smirk and yelled "Amelia!" She smiled and gave me a look that said, "Velcome to the vays of Rossiya, Steef."

My three compartment mates were all very pleasant, and they didn't seem upset by the three-to-one arrangement, although one used sign language to warn me that there will be no hanky-panky here. I immediately dubbed them my Steppe Sisters. Their names were pronounced Galyah, Glavah, and Preemah.

I taught the women how to play Crazy Eights and they caught on swiftly. The other Russians in their group, also extremely friendly, visited the compartment regularly, and we had a party for the next three days. The first night the girls and I all slept with our clothes on. On succeeding nights we took off more and more clothing. If this train had traveled all the way to Paris I suppose we'd all have been sleeping in the raw, there would have been some hanky-panky and I'd be writing this from a gulag somewhere.

One night the train lurched to a halt at some small town and I was shaken from my slumber. I was momentarily disoriented. *Where the hell am I?* I thought. Oh, yeah. I'm on a train in the middle of Russia in a compartment with three Russian women, one of whom snores. Think of it! THREE DAYS in a small train compartment with THREE women! That's like spending NINE days in a small train compartment with ONE woman. And no fooling around. Unbelievable.

Any thoughts I had about Russians being dour, humorless and unfriendly were destroyed on this trip. I found the Russians to be fun-loving, polite and generous. I would walk past a compartment and would hear a voice call "Steef!" A woman would motion me into her compartment, bid me to sit, and hand me a piece of roast chicken, a hard-boiled egg and some bread and a glass of vodka.

Vodka! Did these people consume vodka! Not just a shot or two. They would fill a tumbler about a third full—about four shots worth—offer a toast and VOOM!—down the hatch. They would occasionally clear their palate with a sauce that looked like it was made from currants or some other berries.

The toast was always to "peace." Peace, peace, peace. I wondered why. Then one day I got the Big Clue. Most of these people had lost their fathers during World War II, and some of them lost their mothers as well. And they didn't want anything like this ever to happen to them again. (More than 90 percent of Russian males born in 1922 were killed in the war.)

One evening a group of us gathered into a compartment to discuss life in the United States. Leonid Liubimov, who said he had been a member of the Communist Party for eight years, acted as interpreter. Leonid polled them on the questions to be asked. Then the interview started. The very first question: "How much does it cost to park your car?" At first this might seem like an off-the-wall question. It is not. These Russians had pictures of America's expressways jammed bumper-to-bumper with cars pouring into the cities. "Where did all these cars go?" they wanted to know. And certainly it must cost a lot of money to store them. Using 1960s prices, I tried to explain. "It's thirty cents the first half hour, a dollar for two hours, five dollars all day, but there are weekly and monthly rates." I also said that many workers took buses and subways. Leonid translated. They sat there nodding and clucking away and converting all this into rubles and kopeks.

They also peppered me with questions about life in the United States, about color TV (which they didn't have yet), journalists' pay, types of cars, schools, rents, cost of homes. Like Leonid, many of these people were members of the Communist Party. It was their party membership that resulted in such perks as trips outside the Soviet Union, and many were headed for Poland, East Germany and other parts of the Soviet empire. They were truly proud of their country and its accomplishments, but they were nonetheless curious about life in the West and seemed to be very open-minded about it. Nice people.

And the singing! We would gather at night and sing songs, including one that sounded like "Arrrreeva" (and roll that r) whose melody still comes back to me. We all sang with great gusto. After we finished a song, Leonid said, "Steef! Earss. Earss black." But he was pointing to his eyess. Eyess black? What could that mean? But of course! "Dark Eyes." Dum-de-DUMMMMMM-de-dum. So we sang (hummed) that song.

One day Leonid and I were going over a map of Russia. Leonid pointed to the city of Chita, and said, "Steef! Chita! Like in Tarzan, Chita."

The train pulled into Moscow. We all got our baggage together and left. I bade farewell to the girls. Galyah came up to me and said, "Steef, please to enjoy the rest of your trip. It was nice knowingk you." I felt like a fool. I had nothing in Russian to say to her. So I just shook her hand and wished her well in English. Amelia, the compartment maid, was heart-broken. As we left the train, she stood there with tears pouring down her cheeks. Our little party was over.

I stayed at the Bucharest Hotel, an inexpensive place that, of course, did not have a private bath but was clean and quite charming. The hotel staff was dressed in white, and living there seemed like being in a hospital. From my hotel room window I could see St. Basil's Cathedral across the river and beyond that the Kremlin.

I walked all over this city, around Red Square and the Kremlin. I saw a long line of people waiting to view Vladimir Lenin's embalmed remains. The Russians were preparing to mark the 100th anniversary of Lenin's birth, so this was a popular attraction. It also was free, so I got in line. Soon a beefy security guard approached and said, "Nyet, nyet!" It was my camera. He escorted me to an office where I had to surrender my camera and take a claim check. No pictures of Lenin allowed. Then the guard escorted me back to the line. He was pleasant, almost jovial, about the whole thing. I was beginning to wonder where the ugly Russians were.

Visiting Lenin's tomb is exactly like going to a wake, except there is no grieving widow there to whom you could say "Too bad Vladimir didn't live long enough to see the Packers win the Super Bowl," or something. There was no doubt about it: Lenin was the Soviet Union's Jesus Christ. I waited hours to see him.

I stopped at the United States Embassy, a bright and cheerful place, to get some information and just look around. There was a cartoon posted on a wall. It showed burly Russians in overcoats milling about Red Square. One bumps another and says: "Voice of America . . . 8 o'clock . . . Rosemary Clooney . . . pass it on."

I called the *Chicago Tribune* bureau, where Frank Starr, a former rim mate of mine at the Trib, was chief. He was surprised to hear from me, and insisted I come to his apartment for dinner. I took a cab there. Frank's wife, Hannelore, cooked a superb meal and we had a wonderful evening. Frank said he was sure his apartment was bugged, that his car was bugged and that my hotel room probably was bugged. He said the Russian people regularly listened to Voice of America and seemed to have a good idea what was going on in the West, but that receiving a lot of conflicting reports left them confused. He said the young Russians were getting restless.

Frank seemed to be enjoying himself in Moscow. He provided me with some valuable travel tips. Later he took me in his car to the Ukraine Hotel, where Jim Stewart was staying, and then to my hotel. Classy guy, that Frank! It was a grand evening.

The next evening Jim Stewart and I went out for dinner at the Metropol, where we had champagne and a dinner of—yup!—chicken Kiev and borscht. It was excellent.

I left Moscow on October 8. I took a cab to the Intourist office, where I was to await transportation to the railroad station. I chatted with an Intourist official there. He asked me how things were going on my trip to his country. I said everything was just fine. He seemed happy to hear that. I asked him how I would know which cab to take to the railroad station. He pulled out a piece of paper and wrote a license number on it. It was like something out of a James Bond movie. The cabbie taking me to the station refused a tip, but did accept the half pack of vile Russian cigarettes I handed him.

Leonid Liubimov and many of the other Russians from his group were on this train as well. So we tried to resume our partying. It wasn't quite as lively this time.

We got to the Polish border. While we went through customs, railworkers jacked up the cars and new undercarriages were fitted to accommodate the change in the rail gauge.

The Poles were much like the Russians—jovial, extroverted, fun-loving. The customs official flipped swiftly through my belongings. He found a no-no: a Russian ruble I had slipped inside a book. You are not supposed to take rubles out of Russia. The official looked at me and said, "Souvenir, eh?" closed the book and tossed it aside.

Our next stop was the border with East Germany. I found I had made a dreadful mistake. The East Germans wanted western currency to pay for the transit visa. I had given away dollars and Kennedy half dollars as souvenirs, and now I had almost no western currency except Australian, which they would not accept, and travelers' checks, which they couldn't use either. And those East German customs officials were the surliest people I had encountered on my trip. I needed $1.25 to get through the Berlin Wall to West Berlin. I did something most unusual. With Leonid doing the translating, I borrowed the dollar I had given to a traveler named Viktor as a souvenir. It dawned on me later that I had borrowed a U.S. dollar from a member of the Soviet Communist Party so I could buy my "freedom" from East to West. I later sent Viktor a thank-you note—and enclosed a dollar.

I had to go through customs and then through an inspection at a checkpoint, after which we walked to the other side of the Berlin Wall. It was a tense situation and everyone seemed overly cautious and sometimes mean. The wall had made people ugly. And East Germany was as drab and humorless as the vopos patrolling it.

West Berlin, on the other hand, was bright, colorful, prosperous, and free. You could sense the difference immediately. Never had I been so exposed to such a dramatic life change as that from East Berlin to West Berlin.

I walked down Unter den Linden, widest boulevard I have ever seen, and marveled at the clothing and other goods in the sidewalk display cases. And the colors! Deep reds, purples, whites and blacks. A most prosperous place.

I walked east toward the Berlin Wall, which ran through a large and—at least until the wall ran through it—attractive park. The closer I got to the wall, the more I was struck by the East/West schism. The place became barren and ugly and then downright scary, with barbed wire draped in lines in front of the wall with obstacles scattered here and there to foil would-be escapees and to keep the people off Charottenburger Chausee. The place was strewn with rocks that had been hurled by angry people.

The wall itself was ugly and shoddily built, slapped together in the haste of implementing a bizarre policy. Think of the great walls of history. There's the Wailing Wall, Hadrian's Wall, the Great Wall of China. Wonderful walls, great tourist attractions, especially the Chinese job. And then the Berlin Wall. Bad PR job, that. Not only was it a symbol of tyranny, it was an advertisement that the people of the Communist East don't know how to build walls. If they build walls like this what do their cars look like? Yeah. No self-respecting labor union would have tolerated such a shoddy piece of work. Obviously the Communists don't believe that a job worth doing is worth doing well. No wonder the Communist economy collapsed.

Looking back on it, though, we are most fortunate that the Berlin Wall was built the way it was. Had it been built like the Great Wall of China, the historic preservation geeks would have fought to save the thing. I'm glad I saw the Berlin Wall. I am also delighted it is gone.

The West Germans were wonderful. They reminded me much of Americans. They seemed to care a lot about their new democracy. Now they knew what was going on and they were doing something about it.

The two Germanys were marking the twentieth anniversary of their divorce that year, so there were a lot of flags flying in the German Demokratic Republik (East) and German Federal Republik (West).

After a day in West Berlin, I boarded the train to continue my trip into Western Europe. But I momentarily forgot that West Berlin is an island in the East, and we had to travel through sullen and unhappy East Germany again to get to the real West. I had to pay another $1.25 for a transit visa, but this time I had it, of course. The East German police and customs officials were at their usual unfriendly best. I suppose that for these jobs the East German government purposely recruited people who disliked the West. Otherwise there'd be even more people trying to escape.

I changed trains at Osnabruck, then shot through the rest of Germany, into the Netherlands and to the Hook of Holland where I caught an overnight ferry to Harwich, England.

8

London

An Englishman I met on the ferry gave me the lowdown on British currency, which was confusing. These were the days before Britain converted to the decimal system. So a pound was made up of 20 shillings, and a shilling was worth 12 pence. Try to add up the cost of two items, one worth one pound, 18 shillings and 6 pence, the other worth three pounds, 12 shillings, and 9 pence. You couldn't add this decimally. The currency difficulties drove even the Brits bonkers. And, oh yes, a guinea was one pound and one shilling.

The ferry arrived in Harwich at 6:45 A.M. and I caught a train to Liverpool station, London, seventy-three miles distant. I had traveled from Melbourne to London strictly on the surface, by sea and rail. It was a journey of 11,925 miles.

At Liverpool station I called hotel service and got a nice room, breakfast included, for 35 shillings ($4.20—this was 1969, remember). I bought a map of London, which can be a confusing city because the street names keep changing. But the map of the Underground was easy to understand, and in no time I was zipping all around this great city on the subway trains.

I later transferred to a B&B run by a Romanian couple. I didn't like the usual British fare of greasy eggs for breakfast, so I always ordered hard-boiled eggs. Every time the B&B operator saw me he muttered "Boilingk ex."

The Brits were a great bunch. They were totally indifferent to Americans, and while they knew by our accents that we weren't *them,* they seemed to treat us as equals, not as loud and boorish former colonials, which is, sadly, the way many Americans behave abroad. An Australian woman told me that the world's worst travelers were American women. Loud and spoiled, she said. Complained a lot. Many of the men weren't any different.

I went on a number of tours, saw lexicologist Ben Johnson's digs, visited Charles Dickens' hangouts, including the pub where he wrote much of the *Pickwick Papers.* The city was boundless in its offerings.

Every now and then you would pass a white-pillared house with a brass plaque on the front noting that William Wordsworth or some other famous poet or writer lived there during his productive years. Many of London's streets sounded familiar, as well they should have, because so many of them are in the fairy tales we read as children. I walked all over that great city, and everywhere I turned there was another piece of history popping up. London was simply inexhaustable. I loved it.

I stopped at the *Chicago Tribune* bureau, where I met bureau chief Arthur Veysey and bought a Tribune.

One night in a pub I quaffed a few beers with a group of friendly "dustmen" (trash collectors). They were complaining that they were not allowed to filch items from the trash and sell them on the side "for a few bob." Trash was the property of the borough.

One day I emerged from an Underground and was approached by a young boy. "Can you spare a penny for a guy?" he asked. "What guy?" I asked. "Where is this guy?" The boy took me around a corner where a straw dummy was propped against the wall. Clever. They make a dummy out of straw and then panhandle for it. I was being introduced to an annual British celebration, Guy Fawkes Day. Guy Fawkes was the rebel who tried to blow up Parliament in the infamous Gunpowder Plot of the early 1600s. He was captured, tortured and hanged for his crime. Every year Britain celebrates his day. Children collect money to buy fireworks, which they set off in Trafalgar Square, and they make straw dummies, which they call "guys," and they burn the guys in effigy in honor of the real Guy. Guy Fawkes Day falls on November 5, which is my birthday. So I never forget my birthday.

I gave the lad thruppence.

I also bumped into two women from Melbourne, Trish and Pat. I had known them in Melbourne and knew they were on a world trip. They had spent several weeks on a Greek island, and said their expenses there were only a U.S. dollar a day each for lodging and a dollar each for food. Remember, this was 1969. Nonetheless, many parts of Europe and Asia remain very reasonable, especially those off the beaten path.

I took the Underground to Fleet Street, emerging at Blackfriars, not far from St. Paul's Cathedral. Again, a picturesque area steeped in history. God, I loved this city! I walked to the Reuters office and soon was talking with editors there, including Ron Waataja of Minnesota, whose first question was "Do you know John Larkins?" I was happy that John had supplied me with a letter of introduction. I also was delighted to find that there was an opening on the Western Hemisphere (West Hem) desk, and was told that if I could pass the test, the job was mine. Among the Americans working at Reuters were Jim Foley, Jim Anderson, Lars-Erik Nelson and Sid Doment.

Jack Henry, home editor for Reuters, found out I had worked for the *Chicago Tribune*, and was curious about how the *Tribune*, one of Reuters' key clients in the U.S., regarded the Reuters News Service. I told him that one problem was that Reuters would start out with a bulletin, mark the copy "more to come" and then for half an hour no more copy would come. Reuters delighted in scooping other wire services, including AP and UPI in the United States, and I remember it doing so on one space shot.

But I told Mr. Henry that Reuters often would stick us with a bulletin and it was a long time before they followed up with enough material for a complete story. Mr. Henry nodded and seemed to be well apprised of this problem. I did tell him that Reuters had a reputation for being a hustling news service and their copy was good. Mr. Henry seemed delighted to hear that.

The *Tribune* and some other major U.S. papers carried Reuters because it gained them entree to nations with which the US did not then have relations: Communist China, Cuba, North Vietnam, and North Korea. Reuters also was excellent in Africa.

Most Western journalists use the "inverted pyramid" style of writing. That is, they pack the who, what, when, where, why and how into the first paragraph or two to form what they call the lead (often spelled "lede"). But British journalists tend to meander all over the place, like writers of great classics. So the purpose of the West Hem desk was to rewrite the works of British journalists into the inverted-pyramid style.

The West Hem desk served Reuters clients in the United States and Latin and South America. Rewritten stories would be sent to the Bahamas for translation into Spanish and Portuguese for Reuters markets there.

I took the Reuters test, which lasted three days. I perhaps was overly cautious in my rewrites. Waataja judged my work to be "pretty fair." Not exactly a ringing endorsement. He said Reuters would let me know in a week if they had anything for me. Reuters paid me 19.5 pounds for the tryout. This came to about 47 U.S. dollars.

A week later I got a message from Reuters, sent to my B&B: "Following your recent desk trial here we would like to offer you an engagement. I would be grateful if you would telephone for an appointment when we could discuss details." It was signed Charles Farmer, assistant staff manager. I called immediately and arranged to see him at 3 P.M. that day.

Mr. Farmer looked like the actor Sir John Gielgud. He was very formal. He had my test results and my job application on the desk in front of him. We discussed a few matters. Then he sat back in his chair, brought his hands up, tapped his fingers together and said, "I think Roy Tahs has a place for you, Mr. Maersch." Like a fool, I began to giggle. This was just tooooooooooo British. I apologized, but could not rid myself of my Sheboygan smirk. Mr. Farmer went over the details of the job. He said Reuters paid its British journalists 45 pounds a week, but paid the expatriates, as he called us, 48 pounds a week, figuring we needed a few quid more. I'd get five weeks holiday (vacation) to start—typical of jobs in Commonwealth countries. The *Melbourne Herald* also gave me five weeks.

I was amused by his calling us Americans "expatriates." It sounded slightly quaint, a description more apt to the Hemingway-Fitzgerald-Toklas-Stein group in Paris in the 1920s. Expatriate also sounded somewhat unpatriotic. I never considered myself an expatriate. It sounded like a man without a country.

Mr. Farmer said it would take the Home Office at least four weeks to process my "labour permit." Reuters had to satisfy the government that only foreign journalists could perform these jobs. He said I might as well head back to the States and wait until the permit came through.

I thought about the pay at Reuters. Forty-eight pounds a week in those days amounted to $115. You could get almost twice that in the States. I was going backwards. London is not an inexpensive place to live. The expatriates I talked to at Reuters (all seemed to have beards) doubled up to save expenses, same as I did in Chicago five years before. I was excited about the idea of working in London for Reuters, but not enamored of becoming a starving journalist. This job would have been a dream for a financially secure journalist. It was not difficult work—rewrite, essentially—and London was a smashing city within easy reach of Paris, plus there was a romantic air about it all. Still, $115 a week. I'd have to think it over.

I was getting letters from Margaret. She was excited about my getting a job with Reuters and said she wouldn't mind at all living in London. She had lived there before, loved it, and could easily get a job there as a nurse.

After exploring ways to get to the States—I even tried to book passage on the liner *Queen Elizabeth II*—I arranged to fly to Boston on Pan American. Then I took an overnight bus to Milwaukee, via Chicago, stayed in Milwaukee overnight and headed to Sheboygan.

9

Milwaukee

I stayed with my parents in Sheboygan and took odd jobs until Reuters reported. But then I started to get cold feet. I wasn't sure I wanted to go abroad again. I figured, heck, I was thirty-two, basically I was an American copy editor, I loved the United States and felt that's where I belonged. The Home Office did approve my "labour permit." I pondered the move for a day or so, then decided not to go back. I turned down Reuters and began hunting for a stateside job as a copy editor.

I considered giving the *Milwaukee Sentinel* a rattle to see what kind of a deal I could get from Harry Sonneborn and Harvey SchwandNer. But by this time I much favored afternoon papers, so I called The *Milwaukee Journal* and was immediately connected with Managing Editor Joe Shoquist. He said The Journal had an opening for one copy editor. I arranged for a tryout, took it, passed it, and on Monday, December 22, 1969, I began a stint at The *Milwaukee Journal* that was to last twenty-five years and four months. It was the smartest career move I ever made. Thanks, Joe. My starting pay was $215 a week. And I got one week of vacation. Welcome to America!

My dad, a self-employed tax accountant who had worked sixteen years for the Internal Revenue Service, said that since the *Milwaukee Journal* job was the first one I had since I left the *Melbourne Herald*, I could deduct the travel expenses from Melbourne to Milwaukee—a journey of almost 16,000 miles. The IRS went along with the moving costs. In fact, the trip from Melbourne to Milwaukee cost only about $1,000, so it wasn't that big a deal.

I called Margaret in Australia. I asked her to marry me. She was crying. She said, "Do you really mean that?" I said yes. She was reluctant to leave Australia because of her father's illness. But she agreed she would fly to Milwaukee in a month. Then one day she came home to find her father strapped to his wheelchair and her mother unconscious on the kitchen floor. Her mother had developed an inner ear infection, which turned out not to be very serious. But Margaret was shaken. I now realized that Margaret would never leave Australia. I agreed to fly to Melbourne instead. But the more I got settled in my job at the *Journal* the less I wanted to go abroad again. We wrote each other with passionate regularity, but by April it was no use. We (perhaps I should say I) broke off the engagement. I could have married Margaret had I settled in Australia, but I wasn't sure I could cut it there as a journalist and besides I was beginning to love the *Journal.* It was sad, because I was madly in love with Margaret.

We still exchanged Christmas cards. And for ten years after that, Margaret's mother sent me hand-knit socks at Christmas. Sometimes Margaret's sister-in-law, Sue, sent hand-knit socks, too. I wonder if they were trying to tell me I had gotten cold feet. About a year later Margaret married a doctor. I believe she did the absolutely right thing. I have no doubt that she had a wonderful life.

The *Journal* newsroom was a refreshingly modern environment compared with that of the *Tribune.* There was a woman mid-level editor, Ruth Wilson, and a handful of black staffers. The *Tribune* I left, which was still emerging from its McCormick cocoon, had one black journalist and no female editors. The wisdom behind having all-male editors was that women do not possess the "dirty minds" necessary to keep vulgar and obscene word plays and double entendres out of the paper. This is true. Women generally do not have dirty minds. All men have dirty minds. So we had to train 'em.

The Journal had a much smaller news operation. The staff was considerably younger and more energetic. Also, the *Journal* editorials were moderate to liberal, which suited my views better.

Howard Fibich, the news editor, was a magnificent organizer and also decisive, which made him easy to work for. The rap on him was that he could be difficult at times. One day I thought he was going to murder a copy editor who spelled the police chief's name "Breir" instead of "Breier" in a headline. He was working with a small crew (one Saturday morning I was the lone copy editor on the Local Desk) and somehow managed to squeeze the most out of us.

I didn't know it at the time, but I had the great fortune of landing a job on what was possibly America's finest afternoon newspaper enjoying its last hurrah.

Seven years later Margo Huston, working on an idea put together by Managing Editor Joe Shoquist, would win the Pulitzer Prize for her series on elderly people struggling to remain in their own homes. It was the last Pulitzer won by the *Journal*.

Margo also spearheaded the Journal Women's Group, which championed women's concerns and fought—successfully—to get equal pay for woman journalists. The group also singled out news stories it felt were sexist, and every now and then such a story would appear on the staff bulletin board stamped "This Viewpoint Discriminates Against Women." The Women's Group put a cardboard box atop a bookshelf and invited staffers to submit examples of stories that portrayed women in a poor light. I used to stuff lingerie ads in there. I mean, what could be more degrading than for womenkind to be paraded through the newspapers in their undies? Perhaps it was antics like this that always got me No. 2 on The Journal Women's Group's shit list.

Newspapers were going through a transition in the 1970s. More blacks were appearing in the newsroom and more women were advancing to the copy desks and on to managerial positions. This posed a problem for perpetual grunts like myself. We guys had to develop techniques to deal with woman bosses (many of whom were excellent). I employed one trick. If a female boss berated me for a piece of shoddy work and I felt embarrassed and was trying to defuse her anger I would cup my hands, bow my head and say "Yeth, Mom." Try it, guys. It works!

I had an office mother, Anne Curley of the Business Desk. And when she left I was "adopted" by Janine Ghelfi, a clerk-typist in Entertainment. One Monday in May I came to work, passed Janine and said, "Good morning!" She refused to answer. I sat at my desk. Janine was upset about something. "All right, Janine, what is it?" I asked. "What was yesterday?" she demanded. "Yesterday was Sunday," I said. "Yes, but what day was it?" I thought a minute. "It was Mother's Day." "Well, don't you at least send your mother a card on Mother's Day?" Thorry, Mom.

I also had an office daughter, entertainment writer Tina Maples, and for a time an office son, Kevin Merida. Last I heard, my "son" was working for the Washington Post.

Wisconsin was and is a more progressive place than Illinois, and seems to constantly live up to its motto, "Forward." In fact, Wisconsin is considered one of America's eight trend-setting states, a place where new things happen, especially in education and social areas.

But Milwaukee did have a reputation for being a blue-collar place. A woman told me that when she thought of Minneapolis, she pictured a woman with a rose clenched in her teeth. And when she thought of Milwaukee, she pictured a woman wearing a babushka. That was our last date.

My first impression of the *Journal* newspaper? Clean. Unlike the Chicago papers, the *Journal* managed to produce typo-free editions—although in fairness the cut-throat competition in Chicago caused editors to rush onto the streets with their editions as soon as they could, typos be damned. The *Journal*'s photo staff was outstanding, the art department superb, and the news information center (morgue) was cheerful and accommodating—although the people there had a wacky way of filing things. One editor, looking up Emperor Haile Selassie of Ethiopia, found him filed under "Judah, Lion of."

The paper's headlines were lively and often funny, and I hoped to contribute to this.

I was so giddy about my new job at the *Journal* that on a visit to Sheboygan I boasted to a *Sheboygan Press* reporter that the *Journal* almost never made mistakes. A few days later he sent me a tearsheet from the *Journal*. It contained a two-column story without a headline on it!

The *Journal* had a bowling team called the Chasers, which I quickly joined, and the team shanghaied me into becoming captain. It happened at a party. I went into the kitchen to fetch something, and when I returned, Tom Barber of the Local Copy Desk said, "Did you find what you were looking for, captain?" That's how they went about "electing" team captains. We were terrible bowlers, but we had a lot of fun.

The *Journal* had a staff of about 220, including part-timers. That would make it about a third the size of the *Tribune*'s staff.

The *Journal* was loaded with excellent copy editors. Joining the staff a year after me was Dan Chabot and quickly following him was Carroll Kraus, the quietest and one of the most efficient journalists I have ever known. I think there were weeks in which he uttered but three words. However, in private, Kraus was, in fact, talkative and funny, especially when he did takeoffs on his bosses.

Since I could be a bit of a wizenheimer, I would clash with the guy in the slot or with some other journalist. One day Stu Hoyt, dean of Journal copy editors and usually a mild-mannered person, got angry with me and screamed, "What's the matter? Don't you know anything about English?" Un poquito, Stu, un poquito. Stu could speak about eight languages and read a dozen, including Russian. He translated a letter I received from Leonid Liubimov, the member of the Soviet Communist Party I had met on the Trans-Siberian. I was very impressed! Leonid asked some intriguing questions, such as "Why is Wisconsin called the Badger State?" and "Is Warren Knowles still governor?" I think Leonid may have been a spy! Leonid asked if I could send him a catalogue of fashionable American clothing patterns for his wife. I sent him a huge Penney's catalogue. I never got a reply, so I don't know whether Leonid received it.

Stu married a delightful blonde metro desk secretary named Maggie, who was born in the United States but raised in England, which left her with a delightful English accent. She resembled the socialite/actress Dina Merrill and had more design ideas than Martha Stewart.

The copy desk had a group called NARM, the National Association of Rim Men (later Members), founded by Tom Barber. NARM would hold a picnic each summer. At one of these events Stu and Maggie showed up with a white tablecloth that they draped on the grass. Then they placed expensive silver and china on the tablecloth, broke out their picnic lunch and sat down to feast. I wonder how many NARMies realized that Stu and Maggie were recreating a scene from "Citizen Kane."

Stu and Maggie lived in a Victorian-style home on Van Buren Street. Maggie decorated the place in Victorian splendor, then would invite us lucky staffers over for Christmas parties. It was like visiting an 1880s English manor. Magnificent. You expected Charles Dickens to emerge from a room any minute.

Milwaukee had the oldest continually operating press club in the nation and it held an annual contest for print and electronic journalists. I was delighted to find that there was a contest for headline-writing. I entered this contest twenty-three times and won it fourteen.

I found a few problems at the *Journal.* Unlike those at the *Chicago Tribune*, the Journal writers were not potty-trained on style. Yet the *Journal* was fussy about its style rules, in particular the that-which rule (clue: which is almost always preceded by a comma) and the sequence-of-tense rule (says . . . will/said . . . would—no exceptions!). But the *Journal* turned the job of enforcing the rules over to the copy editors. This might seem minor, but we copy editors ended up correcting the same style-rule violations day after day, week after week—same same same. It got downright fatiguing.

I felt that if the style rules were important, they should be taught to EVERYONE, not just the copy editors. And enforce the rules. Either that or throw the stylebook out the window and go wild. Not a terrible idea either. Style-persnickety papers run the risk of becoming comma-wise and libel foolish. I was always afraid that someday something like this might happen: "Well, yes, Your Honor, we admit we called the plaintiff a son-of-a-bitch—but we hyphenated it correctly!"

Copy editors should be reading for sense. Misspelled words, misspelled names, style-rule violations and other slop has no business being there. Professional journalists should not dump garbage on the desks of other professional journalists.

The copy editor's life seems to be one never-ending stream of verbosity, redundancy, superfluosity, dangling modifiers, non sequiturs, inelegant truncations, inadvertent suturizations, and downright gibberish. And that doesn't include stories with huge holes or with libelous matter. But, such was life on the desk. The writers got to be the Great Circus Parade and the copy editors got to pick up the poop.

Sad fact is, there are not very many good writers out there, and the nation's best writers do not necessarily end up in journalism, but in more lucrative fields. My Uncle Carl was a wonderful, Buchwald-style humorist who could have had a career as a humor columnist. He instead became a dentist. But on the side he wrote the most hilarious letters I have ever read.

Some of the writers on the *Journal* were superb, and I marveled at their work. But as with all papers, the *Journal* had its share of impossible writers, people who could barely create two paragraphs without starting a grammatical civil war. And yes, there are journalists who owe their careers to the work of copy editors. You bet!

The *Journal* had a few slobs, writers who would vomit their egos into the system and send the mess on to the copy desk, apparently with the view that it was the copy editor's job to make the result palatable to readers.

It was like someone dumping a bucket of garbage in your lap and saying "Clean it up!" I once got up from the Local Copy Desk in disgust and said, "We're supposed to be copy editors, not garbage collectors."

I thought the *Journal* was lax in quarantining the slobs. I didn't mind a bit of slop here and there, especially in stuff written under deadline pressure, but a lot of this stuff was not written under deadline pressure. With some of these writers it was like cleaning the Aegean Stables. It's no wonder the *Journal*—and a lot of other papers—find it hard to get good copy editors. Who wants to be a garbage collector?

A newspaper's copy editors are like journalism professors whose classes never let out. The copy editors know the writers backwards and forwards. After a while we could tell not only what error a writer would make, but when he would make it. On occasion, during down times, we copy editors would cattily rank the writers, the ten best and ten worst. Then we would compare our lists. I was amazed not only that the same writers made the lists, but in some cases in the same order.

On the other hand, some *Journal* writers were so good that at times I would forget I was supposed to edit their work and instead sat there in awe of it. Should I be so daring as to name my favorite writers over the years? Of course. Outstanding were Don Pfarrer and Jerry Kloss. Others whose work I loved to edit were Jim Spaulding, Dick Kenyon, Dave Offer, Margo Huston, Doug Armstrong, Dave Umhoefer, Joanne Weintraub, Thor Christensen, Bob Wells, Wynn Delacoma, Eugene Kane, Jacquelyn Mitchard, Lois Blinkhorn, Tom Strini, Jackie Loohauis—and a few more that I surely missed.

Naturally, I have some ideas on how to handle disobedient writers. For instance, the chronic style-rule violators. First, make up a list of the twenty-five style rules most commonly violated. Give each writer two copies—one for work and one for home. Hold a meeting in the newsroom. Tell the writers that in order to take pressure off the copy editors, especially on deadline, the editors were from now on going to expect that the writers will follow these style rules. The writing coach will help if needed. Then go to it.

The copy editors would keep track of those following style rules and would send them thank-you notes for their cooperation. Those who failed or refused to follow style would be "listed." One day two copy editors would pay a visit to the No. 1 violator. One copy editor would say, "Well, since you don't wish to be potty-trained on style, perhaps you could use one of these." Then—plumpf-ff!—the second copy editor would toss a disposable diaper on the offender's desk. I think the problem of style-rule violations could be cleared up with . . . oh . . . I think a couple cases of Pampers ought to do it.

The terrible writers and slobs should be treated far more harshly. They should be discreetly identified. Their problems should be noted, and the copy editors should be specific. Then they should be turned over to the editor her/himself. The editor, along with the writing coach, would work with them. They would be told in no uncertain terms that their work would have to improve, and if it didn't—well. It's a lot harder to find a good copy editor than a sloppy writer. Amen! Slobs are copy-editor killers.

Meanwhile, the more I worked at the *Journal* the more I realized that Wisconsin was a more modern and open place than Illinois. I cite four examples:

The Equal Rights Amendment: The people of Wisconsin have long held that women do indeed have souls and thus are equal to males in the eyes of God and man. The people of Illinois have a lot of trouble with such a radical concept. So when the Equal Rights Amendment was sent to the states for ratification, the Wisconsin Legislature had no trouble with it and voted to ratify. But the Illinois Legislature, probably in deference to Favorite Daughter Phyllis Schlafly, joined the Deep South and rejected it. The ERA fell three votes shy of ratification, and my guess is that if Illinois had supported it two other states would have fallen in line and the ERA would be part of the Constitution.

Feelthy Movies: The people of Wisconsin believe that if you want to harm your soul by watching feelthy movies, that's your business. So when the feelthy movie "Deep Throat" came out in the mid-70s, a theater on Lisbon Avenue screened it. Many Journal staffers saw "Deep Throat" (yep, I did), including two female staffers who showed up wearing dark glasses. (And I'd DIE before I would name them.) But "Deep Throat" was banned in Boss Town, as Chicago was sometimes known in those days because of Mayor Richard J. (Boss) Daley.

Sports Venues: The Green Bay Packers play in Lambeau Field, a marvelous facility designed strictly for football. The seating is so good that fans can get a generous view of the action from almost anywhere. National Football League players love it, saying it reminds them of college stadiums.

Meanwhile, the Chicago Bears, representing a city thirty times larger than Green Bay and presumably thirty times richer, play in a monstrosity called Soldier Field that is more appropriate for chariot racing than football. What Chicago should do is tear down the eyesore, use the rubble to build a parking lot in Lake Michigan and give its fans a REAL football stadium. Certainly the Frank Lloyd Wright school in Spring Green, Wisconsin, could help.

Instead, Chicago has decided to renovate the relic. Renovate Soldier Field? That makes as much sense as installing cruise control in a 1924 Hupmobile.

And then there's Miller Park, which is far superior to any baseball stadium in Chicago. It appears that Chicago, with all its money, is perfectly content to live in the shadow of Green Bay and Milwaukee when it comes to sports venues.

The Chicago Swagger. Every year the Milwaukee Press Club holds its Gridiron Dinner, at which it awards prizes to members of the print and electronic media. A prominent journalist or media executive is chosen to receive the Press Club's Sacred Cat Award, and this person speaks at the event. (The Sacred Cat Award is named after the remains of a cat found between two downtown Milwaukee buildings being torn down.)

Over the years, Gridiron Dinner attendees have enjoyed the privilege of hearing such luminaries as Helen Thomas, Peter Arnett, Louis Rukeyser, Malcolm Forbes, Ted Turner, Reuven Frank, Walter Cronkite, Art Buchwald, Paul Gigot and Judy Woodruff. These speakers were gracious (Woodruff), inspiring (Cronkite) and hilariously funny (Buchwald).

There was one exception: A *Chicago Sun-Times* columnist and TV personality. He insulted the award, said the Press Club merely used it so it could get a speaker for its dinner. This is essentially true, but you're not supposed to say that. And anyway, if he thought the award was beneath him he should have refused it. He made it sound as though he was doing all of us a great favor by traveling ninety miles north to talk to us. And after his crummy speech, His Royal Highness condescended to appear at the Press Club, where he carried on like Mussolini reviewing his troops.

It amazed me that anyone would behave like that, especially one from a comparatively backward state like Illinois. And Chicago, an attractive city with a passion for corruption, is just what former *Milwaukee Journal* writer Carl Sandburg called it: "A lady with dirty underwear."

I was delighted that the Press Club had an award for headlines, and I was determined to go after it. Entrants could submit their six best heds for the year, with enough copy attached to make sure the heds weren't too wide of the mark (heh heh). I won the contest a few times and was developing the swagger of the regular winner. But one year a female leg darted out in front of me and I tripped over it. Dorothy Holm of the *Milwaukee Sentinel* won the headline award. But then I reeled it off five times in a row and eight times out of nine. Dan Chabot, an editor on the National Desk and a better headline writer than I, stopped me. I think it was Dan's hed on a story about a burglary in an Italian perfume factory that did it. I could write heds for a thousand years before coming up with Chabot's gem: "Arrivederci aroma."

Other winners of the headline award in my time or before it were Len Scheller, Tom Barber, Russ Austin, Dom Noth, Pat Reardon, Steve Byers, Joan Grosz and Jim Price of the *Journal*; Dorothy Holm and Cathy Jakicic of the *Sentinel*; Doug Larson of the *Green Bay Press Gazette* (who also supplied us with hundreds of those witty Green Sheet overlines), Maureen Macozzi and Dean Robbins of Madison's *Isthmus Magazine*, and Tom Paquin of the *Eau Claire Leader-Telegram*.

The *Journal* newsroom and composing department became computerized in 1976. We all wondered what would happen with our work. Would it improve because of the speed? Would it be the same? It was the same. Now, instead of sending our garbage by truck we were sending it by jet. Under the hot-lead system, it would take more than forty minutes to have a piece of copy print-ready for the paper. The electronic system reduced this to seven minutes.

There were a few characters in our newsroom.

There was the vesuvial Harvey Peacock, of course, and Len Scheller of the Local Copy Desk, writer Ray McBride, Tom Lubenow, sometime police reporter and metro editor, and Walter Monfried, who had a phobia for germs.

McBride had a wonderful way of dealing with testy callers. If they called screaming about something in the paper, he could calm them down by talking to them quietly and promising "I will take a memo on that." That usually pacified them. If they continued ranting, Ray would let them carry on and at the point where they would have to take a breath he would leap in and say, "I think you are absolutely correct. What we are going to . . . " and disconnect in mid-sentence, leaving the irate caller believing that it was the phone company responsible for the cutoff, not Ray. Gennie McBride, Ray's daughter, said Ray used such techniques in dealing with Mrs. McBride.

Lubenow was a crack reporter and later a metro editor. One day I was editing a story about a pending firefighters' strike. I went to Lubey and said, "Didn't the firefighters go on strike about five years ago? And shouldn't we note that in the story?" Lubey says, "I think you're right. Let's go." He got up to head toward the News Information Center. But on the way he grabbed a phone and dialed a number from memory. "Hey, Frank," he said. "When's the last time you guys walked?" He got the information, relayed it to me, and that was that.

Milwaukee seems like the last place on earth to have a riot, but it did have an uprising in the black neighborhoods in 1967. Lubey, then a police reporter, was among the journalists covering it. Also in town were FBI agents. A few years later the *Journal*, under the Freedom of Information Act, demanded to know what kind of information the FBI gathered on *Journal* reporters. All the FBI report said about Lubey was, "Just a foul-mouthed police reporter." Lubey saw that and said, "Why, those mother————s!" Well, the FBI got that one right. I don't think Lubey minded being called a foul-mouth; I think he was upset by the brevity of the report. It should have noted that he was a crack reporter, a member of the Sheboygan Mafia (staffers born or raised in Sheboygan), devoted husband and father, and he loved brats and especially beer. He kept a keg permanently on tap in his garage.

One day Lubey tumbled to the floor in the office. Brain tumor. He was gone in less than four months. He was fifty-four. Journalism had lost a great one.

Walter Monfried, who used to motor around the building humming arias from his favorite operas, had a germ phobia. He would enter the men's room, using his elbows to open the door, then do his duty. After that he would scrub down like a surgeon, then stand at the exit door until someone came along to open it so he could get out. It was difficult at first to believe that there was a person like this, but sure enough, on more than one occasion I would enter the john and see Walter standing there, hands raised, waiting for someone to leave so he could follow.

Journalists also could be nasty people. The cafeteria was on the same floor as the newsroom. If a reporter or editor were needed in the newsroom, a call would be placed to the cashier, and the woman on duty, often an aging lady, would grab the nearby microphone and call out in her quaky-shaky voice, "Bob Barewald!" The journalists loved that voice so much they did dastardly things to hear it. So, one day, I am dining and I hear "the voice" call out "Martin Bormann." Couple days later, it was "Reinhard Heydrich." And then "Heinrich Himmler." Finally, "Hermann Goering." But by this time "the voice" caught on and said, "There's nobody here by that name." As I say, journalists can be nasty people.

10

Journal Stock

Journal Communications, Inc. is employee-owned. Or that is to say, 91 percent of the stock is owned by the employees, the other 9 percent by the descendants of the original owners. The descendants own the original shares, the employees own shares broken down into "units".

The deal is this: After you are employed by the company for six months (used to be three years) and whether full or part time, you can buy Journal Communications stock. You only have to put 20 percent down and you can borrow the other 80 percent at a major downtown bank or at the Journal Credit Union.

We used to get stock loans at the prime rate—the rate banks charge their preferred customers. Now this rate has been reduced to 0.6 points under the prime. The prime rate currently is 4.75 percent, so banks are lending money for *Journal* stock at only 4.15 percent.

When I started at *The Milwaukee Journal* in 1969 my knowledge of finances was so awful I thought an asset was a female donkey. I never expected to get wealthy as a journalist, but that I would work till age sixty-five and retire on a meager pension and Social Security. Journalists are not highly paid people. In fact, they are paid about a much as schoolteachers, considerably less on a per-hour basis.

I once calculated that, based on the salary I was making when I started at *the Journal*—$11,180 a year—if I saved 5 percent of my income and got a 5 percent return it would take me twenty-one months, or about 630 days, to acquire $1,000. Twenty five years later, thanks to *Journal* stock, I had reduced this time period to $1,000 every five days.

Employee-ownership was the brainchild of a wonderful man named Harry J. Grant, who set up the *Journal* Employees Stock Trust Agreement (JESTA) in May 1937 when he was chairman of the board. Originally, employees had to sell their stock back to the company upon leaving or retiring. This was gradually expanded to ten years for retirees, with the first sale, of one-tenth of the stock, beginning on the first anniversary of the retirement date. Those who quit had to unload all their stock at once.

The company kept the stock dividends fairly high —around 5 percent—which helped employees buy more stock and also handle their loans. *Journal* employees were in a position to retire early and comfortably.

Then, in the spring of 1973, the company introduced a profit-sharing program in which employees could contribute 5 percent of their pay and the company would chip in 40 percent of this amount. The money would be put into an investment fund. The employees could draw out their own taxed contributions to buy *Journal* stock. To get the thing going, the company would contribute one week's pay for each employee.

When a company introduces a plan like this, we get an idea of people's attitude toward finances. To the best of my knowledge, about one-fifth of the employees failed to take advantage of this offer—including a financial writer who was to be on the board overseeing the investments! You can lead a horse to water, but . . .

I did the number-crunching and signed up immediately. I like free money. I talked to one journalist who hadn't signed up for profit-sharing. I asked her why. She said she wanted to pay her bills first. I asked what interest rate she was being charged on the bills. She said most were 18 percent. I asked her what kind of a return she would be getting under profit-sharing. She said she didn't know. I said it was 40 percent with the company contribution, and then if the company got a 6 percent return on its investments, the full return would be 46 percent. She signed up.

By the time I got my first stock offer, in February 1973, I had saved up a little over $800. I bought 100 units for $3,855, borrowing $3,055 from the Marine Bank (now Bank One). I took advantage of three more stock offers, and by the end of that year I owned $10,087 worth of *Journal* stock. My salary at the time was $16,000 a year.

I was paying the interest on the stock loan out of pocket. And even though I was single, the stock loan was putting a big strain on my budget. I was paying $250 a quarter for the interest. In addition I was putting 5% of my income into the profit-sharing plan. By 1975, despite profit-sharing's help, things were getting tight. I hated doing it, but I cut one stock offer in half and turned another offer down flat.

I went to the stock office and got all the information on Journal stock I could, then grabbed my calculator and spent a weekend doing a Benjamin Graham-style securities analysis. What I discovered was:

Journal stock never had a losing year. Its worst year was in the strike-bruising year of 1962 when the total return (growth and dividends) came to 7.15 percent. The company's best year (which still holds) was 1939, when the total return was 28.06 percent. The average total return since 1937 was 15 percent. *Journal* stock has maintained that average. I shook my head. "You've got to buy as much of this stock as possible," I told myself. But how?

When you're having financial problems, the best thing to do is consult the wizards. But Warren Buffett, John C. Bogle and Peter Lynch weren't available, so I chose Jim Conklin of the *Journal* Picture Desk and Bill Manly, the Home Section editor (and brother of the *Chicago Tribune*'s Chesly Manly). Conklin and Manly said they didn't pay the interest on their stock loans out of pocket, but let the dividends take care of that. I didn't know this was possible. I talked with my banker, Barry Dukes, and asked if I could pay the interest from the dividends. "No," he said. "The stock is 'pledged' to the bank." This means that the bank must use the dividends only to reduce the debt. "However . . . " And his "However" opened the door to a financial decision that would be worth at least a half million. "However, what you can do is this: After we have taken the dividends and used them to pay down your loan, you can bring your interest bill to the bank and we will add that onto the loan." "You would do something like that?" I asked. "Yes," he said. "All we care is that your stock equity is 20 percent or better."

Some banks will not go along with such an arrangement, calling it an "evergreen loan." I was glad I was banking at the Marine. So, every quarter for the next eight years I walked to the bank, interest bill in hand, and the bank would add this to my stock loan. Now I could buy all the stock I was offered.

As a result, four things happened, all dramatically. Gross worth went up, net worth went up, debt went up, and taxes went down because I was getting huge write-offs from the interest payments. I remember looking at my books one day in 1979 and realizing that my *Journal* stock loan was more than five times my annual salary. By the time I retired from the *Journal* the loan had grown to eleven times my salary.

I have tried to calculate what kind of overall return I was getting on *Journal* stock. I figured the investment was a thirty-bagger. That is, I was getting $30 back for every dollar I invested. But that was just a part of it. If you're making $35,000 a year and are throwing an interest deduction of, say, $25,000 against it, you are doing a Muhammad Ali job on your taxes. Factor that in and you can add another ten bags to the return.

But there was even more. I borrowed $48,000 against the stock to make a down payment on a house, I borrowed $35,000 to help some nephews and a niece with college, and borrowed to make improvements to my home and for other things. All told, I borrowed out almost six times more than I invested—and didn't repay it, of course. I just continued paying interest on the loan and deducting that from my taxes. So what's my true return on *Journal* stock? Darned if I know.

A champion of the employee-ownership plan and also a source of information was Warren Heyse, then publisher. He had a framed painting of a pair of hands with the caption "God Bless Our Journal Stock." I got a copy of that painting and had it framed and placed in the Journal newsroom. I think it's still there.

Financial advisers warn against owning too much stock in the company you work for, and for good reason. If the company goes belly up you are in deep doodoo. True. What do Kimberly-Clark, Coca-Cola, Walt Disney Company, Dayton-Hudson, PepsiCo, Mobil, Gillette, Avon, Sears and Xerox all have in common? Their stock declined by 60% or more during some period of the 1970s and 1980s. The stocks came bouncing back, but if you retired with a portfolio loaded with such stock and were using it for income you wouldn't bounce back with it. All those, of course, are publicly traded stocks with prices determined by the market. The price of *Journal* stock, which is not publicly traded, is determined by the company itself using a rather complicated formula.

Do employees rush to buy *Journal* stock? It isn't exactly a stampede. One journalist told me he thought owning company stock was a conflict of interest! Other employees would buy the stock strictly cash on the barrelhead. Others would hold their stock loans to 50 percent of the stock's value. And then there were the "plungers" like myself. I once even borrowed against MasterCard to get cash to buy stock. When I told Managing Editor Joe Shoquist about this, he said "Don't do that!" But it paid off. I was just playing the percentages.

I loved to calculate the return on *Journal* stock using various scenarios. Let's say it's a normal year in which the stock appreciates 10 percent and dividends are 5 percent. An employee is offered $10,000 worth of stock and buys it for cash. The gross total return is 15 percent. Then if the employee should sell the stock, she would have to pay 20 percent taxes on the $1,000 capital gain or $200, and 28 percent income taxes on the $500 in dividends, or $140. So the net return on equity (ROE) comes to $1,160, or 11.6 percent.

The person buying the stock half down, half borrowed at a rate of 6 percent produces a more interesting scenario. Five thousand down, $5,000 borrowed at 6 percent. Total return $1,500. Out of this the stock owner has to pay $300 in interest, $220 in capital gains taxes and $140 in income taxes on the dividends. But the $300 in interest is deductible, and assuming a 28 percent income bracket, means a net outlay for interest of $216. So we have a total return of $1,500 minus $200, minus $140, minus $216 for $944. Divide that by the $5,000 ventured, and ROE is 18.8 percent.

Now take the person who puts down $2,000 and borrows $8,000 at 6 percent. Total return is $1,500. Taxes are the same as above, $200 on capital gains, $140 on dividends. Interest on the loan comes to $480, minus 28 percent for $346. Run that through your calculator and you get an after-tax return of $814 and ROE of 40.7 percent ($814 divided by $2,000 ventured). And that's how fortunes are made. The returns are strikingly more dramatic in years when the total return is more than 20 percent. And that has happened several times.

And, of course, those who buy heavily on margin can take the cash they otherwise would have used and invest it somewhere else.

One day I got a call from Tom Pavek, my mole in the Production Department.

"Steve!"

"Yeah."

"Did you ever think of unpledging some of your *Journal* units and using the dividends to contribute to a 401(k)?"

No, I had never thought of that. So with Tom's help, I set it up. I had plenty of dividends to take care of the stock loan, so all this amounted to was a shifting of assets from one pile to another. No out-of-pocket requirements.

Talk about saving for retirement. I was buying all the *Journal* stock I was offered, I was contributing 5 percent of income to the *Journal* profit-sharing program, I was contributing $2,000 a year to my IRA, another $2,000 a year (or so) to a 401(k), I was destined to receive a company pension, and I also qualified for Social Security.

But I didn't venture into the 401(k) plan without hearing Samuel Insull screaming from his grave, "What'd

I do? What'd I do?'' If *Journal* Communications ever went belly up the lines of its stockholders would wrap themselves several times around bankruptcy court. But the company remains strong even through 2002's economic turmoil.

Borrowing heavily for stock can create some problems. During the stagflation of the early 1980s the prime rate went above 20 percent. JournalComm managed to get the banks to hold the rate on Journal stock loans to 15 percent, but some unitholders faced a 1929-style "call" and had to unload stock so they could pay the interest on the debt and keep their equity above 20 percent. It was a disturbing time, and we all watched our loans carefully. However, the economy eventually righted itself. I continued buying stock through the bad times.

The *Journal* stock plan allowed me to become financially independent, though I didn't become a millionaire. I retired when the *Journal* and *Sentinel* merged. Had I been able to hang on a few more years, I might have become a millionaire. Many others did. I talked to a recent retiree, two years younger than myself, who had been with the company thirty-five years. "How much *Journal* stock did you end up with?" I asked. "A little over $3 million," he said. Not bad for a guy who probably never made more than $65,000 a year. I didn't ask how much debt he was carrying, but I wouldn't be surprised if it were $1.5 million.

It is not unusual these days for JournalComm employees with thirty years service to retire as millionaires. Of course, there is a caveat to this. As the doctor once stated in his column: "You will probably survive your myocardial infarction provided you don't die suddenly in the first few weeks." So, too, JournalComm should tell its employees: "Thanks to *Journal* stock, you probably will enjoy a most comfortable retirement—provided that one day we don't haul you down to a third-floor office and have you liquidated."

The *Journal* stock plan was run by JESTA—*Journal* Employees Stock Trust Agreement. Messages from JESTA would appear periodically on the staff bulletin board. One day such a message went up. I typed out a sentence and placed it under that. "This message brought to you by the *Journal* Employee's Stock Trust Agreement Policy Organization—JESTAPO." Such levity was not greeted warmly, and my little note was stripped from the board almost immediately.

What helped me get my financial course set properly was the use of budget cards to coincide with biweekly paydays. I did this initially to organize my bill-paying, so I would not have late payments. I continue to use this record-keeping system in retirement. It requires only minutes and I would recommend it to anyone.

On the blank side of an index card I noted the date of the payday, including year. Then I would list all bills due that payday (mortage, electricity, heat, insurance, credit cards, etc.), making sure there was enough in my checking account to cover them. On the reverse side, on the left, I would list assets—*Journal* stock, profit-sharing, savings accounts, checking account, other investments—but not the value of my home or car. Opposite that I would list debits—the *Journal* stock loan, mortgage, car loan, consumer loans. Each payday I would subtract the debits from the assets to get a rough calculation of net worth. At the end of the year I would add the value of my home to the mix, based on the estimated market value provided on the property tax bill. Then I would tally up my financial situation. It was absolutely delightful to go over the books at the end of each year and discover that net worth was increasing at a sum substantially greater than annual salary.

Of course, we are not on this Earth to smear ourselves with the excrement of our wealth. Tom McCollow, chairman of the board, came up with a nice way to dispense with our surplus riches in 1986 by forming the *Journal* Foundation as part of the Milwaukee Foundation. He noted that the tax laws would change in 1987 and write-offs for charitable donations would be reduced. So in the nick of time, in December of 1986, he put forth a plan for officers and employees of the company to contribute $25,000 worth of *Journal* stock to a donor-advised fund. I talked this over with my dad, Fred, who enjoyed a career as a banker, Internal Revenue Service agent and self-employed tax accountant. He had long been after me to give more to charity, so when he saw this *Journal* Foundation plan he wrestled me to the floor and twisted my arm until I promised to sign up. (I exaggerate.)

A $25,000 donation was a big hit against my net worth, but I figured I could turn my entire charitable program over to it so I would no longer have to dip into other income sources for charity. It all made sense.

McCollow then set up the *Journal* Foundation Advisory Committee. He was elected chair. Warren Heyse, then president of the company, was elected vice chair and I was elected secretary. I still am.

The $25,000 donation? I got a $7,000 write-off, spread over two years. This after-tax contribution of $18,000 has grown to $92,000 and has already produced more than $30,000 for charity. I could not recommend the *Journal* Foundation/Milwaukee Foundation strongly enough. Call the Greater Milwaukee Foundation at (414) 272-5805 and do it. Or check them out at www.greatermilwaukee-foundation.org. (Now if only the Milwaukee Foundation could spell Harvey Schwandner correctly!)

If you live in some other city, check out the charitable foundations there. But give generously. You get to sleep the sleep of the just.

11

Heds

Headline writers are always looking for short, snappy verbs to use in their heds, as we call them. Words like rip, rap, hit, slap, flay, assail, blast, irk. I had a brief love affair with the word ooze. As in "Sewage bill oozes through council." I mean . . . can't you just *see* it?

I was always on the lookout for fresh words I could use in headlines. One day, whilst reading a British publication, I stumbled across the word higgledy-piggledy. When's the last time you saw that word in a headline? Don't blame me. One fortnight later: "Planner decries higgledy-piggledy zoning."

When I started at the *Journal* in 1969 I was delighted to find that the Milwaukee Press Club had a contest for headline writing.

Do I have suggestions on writing heds? Hah!

1. Get off the who, what, when, where, why, how carousel as quickly as possible. Too many "Me Tarzan, you Jane" heds in there.
2. Look at the world from different angles. Picasso made a fortune doing that. However, Picasso might not be a good example. His women looked like they had been shoved sideways into a guillotine.
3. Barbara Baird, a clerk typist in the Entertainment Department, referred to headlines as "titles." Yes! Don't write a hed for your story. Write a title.
4. Use a quote. Go into the story and pluck an appropriate quote from it and use that as the hed.

5. Cut and cover. You dip down into the story, find a marvelous phrase, pluck it out and use that as the hed. Then go back, cover up your larceny and stay clear of the writer for a few days.

6. Let the "art" (photos, maps, diagrams, graphs) work for you. For example, if you're dealing with a story about Thomas Edison and the layout contains pictures of Edison you don't have to use his name in the hed. We once ran a story in the Green Sheet about Edison's messy laboratory. The hed I came up with was simply "Tom, about your lab . . . ".

7. Get poetic. My favorite heds are not the usual punners, but the poetic ones. They say the poet defines God's way to man. Well, the journalist defines man's way to man. One of my favorite heds was: "The shah: 'Light of Iran' lives in the shadows."

8. Stay in the English language. Some 70 percent of the words of the English language come from Latin. Avoid them. Stay in English. "Higgledy-piggledy" is English. "Multiculturalism" ain't.

9. Create bag heds. You write headlines ahead of time. Then when the appropriate story comes along, you reach into your bag of pre-written heds and—ta-da!—look at all the time you save. At The Journal I had a large bag of pre-written heds. "A pretty grill is like a melody" and "A site for soirees" found homes. Remaining in the orphanage were (are) "Great balsa fire," "Close, but no Seeger," "Reach out and torch someone" and "This little piggy went to Marquette." (Dan Chabot, who later did a wonderful job as editor of the Green Sheet, retired in tears because he never got to use his "Sault Sioux Sue Soo." He let me borrow his bag hed "Come see, come saw.")

I always found that heds—the wacky ones, any-way—came swiftly or not at all. Like the one on the disco-toga party at UWM: "They were dancing sheet to sheet." It was like a flashbulb going off. If the hed didn't arrive in seconds, it probably never arrived, and you ended up with a very pedestrian hed.

At that time we were using a lot of what I called "Hiroshima heds." These would involve a 48-point hed of just a few words and then a 24-point underline. I feasted on them. Some of my favorites: A prison break in Mexico foiled by an obese inmate: "Pauncho." An old church transformed into a service station: "Amazing grease." Then there was the story by *Journal* writer Barbara Koppe who had fed her unsuspecting husband, Greg, dishes made with horsemeat (they're still married!). A story like that is what hed writers call a "given." I came up with the hed in seconds, and I'm sure most of you readers would, too. I have printed the answer at the end of this chapter. Betcha you came up with the same thing I did.

And sometimes heds don't come so fast. I once was editing a story about Milwaukee police officers who, while on duty, stopped to buy sweet corn for an officers' picnic. (Big Milwaukee police scandal!) I knew there was a neat hed in there, but I couldn't come up with it so I put a pedestrian hed on the story. But it bothered me. I don't like to miss a hed opportunity any more than Jack Nicklaus likes to miss a three-foot putt. It bothered me for a long time. Then one day while driving home to Mequon it came to me. Next day I told Sue Ryon, chief of the Local Copy Desk, about the hed. She says, "But, Steve, the deadline was . . . " Yes, I know. But I think it's a shame to let a good hed to go to waste. Someday I would like to see something like this in the paper:

Pardon the Delay

Two years ago The Journal ran a story about Milwaukee
police officers who, while on duty, purchased sweet corn
for an officers' picnic. The copy editor failed to come up
with a snappy hed for that story. Today he informed us
that he has THE hed. And we'd like to share it with you:
"Corn on the cop."
Thank you for your patience.

Hed writers have a big advantage over writers because they get to scream at the world in huge type, sometimes type three inches tall, while the writers whisper at
the world in 10- or 11-point. But writers get bylines, while
hed writers dance on a stage with the curtain closed.
I had tons of fun doing wacky heds for the Green
Sheet, even on Ann Landers' columns. ("Boyfriend's into
bondage, and she's fit to be tied.") Chabot always managed to pick the features that allowed for mirthful play.
One such story was about Elvis Presley films, which always seemed to involve feasts of one kind or another—barbecues, clambakes, smorgasbords. For a hed I
wrote, "Love me, medium rare." This resulted in an angry
call from an Elvis fan, who thought that was disrespectful
of the King. Come on. Isn't Elvis the guy who gave us the
song "You Ain't Nuthin' but a Hound Dog"?
Answer: "Horse d'ouvres."

12

Blunders

Yeah, we make blunders. We make some beauties. One of the most awful memories I have of newspapering was to read the first edition of the paper and come across an error—mine—that would require a change for the second edition and might require a Setting It Straight as well. You would sit there, staring at your error, and you could feel the building tremble as the presses copied it 150,000 times—enough to misinform 450,000 readers at three readers per paper, a totally rotten feeling.

Our alert composing and press rooms saved us from many a blunder.

When we journalists made an error we had to produce a report for Managing Editor Joe Shoquist explaining how such a thing could happen. We hated to do that. Too many of those could result in a career-threatening situation.

The *Journal* used to run its corrections under the hed "Setting It Straight." The Tribune used to use "Beg Your Pardon." I would prefer "Oops!" or "Oops There." But perhaps "Oops" doesn't sound so good in court. Today the *Journal* and most other papers simply use "Correction," or, on a bad day, "Corrections." I don't know why the paper dropped "Setting It Straight." Possibly some journalist misidentified Charlie's saloon as a gay bar, and the editors didn't like the resulting pun.

In March 1970 the *Journal*'s Sunday *Wisconsin Magazine* carried an interview with a local artist, who produced his own illustrations. One illustration was a self-portrait. The artist's head was framed with a squiggly outline containing a bunch of seemingly indecipherable characters. The Sunday magazine was pre-printed at a plant elsewhere, then shipped to the *Journal* for insertion into the Sunday editions. The preprints began arriving and were stored on skids in the circulation department.

One day an editor was perusing one of these sections. He gazed at the artist's handiwork. He pored over those indecipherable characters that framed the artist's self-portrait. Oh, my God!!! If you held the page a certain way you could see that the characters spelled out "F- - K ALL CENSORS."

What to do.

The editor, Dick Leonard, decided to bring in teams of people to tear out the offending page. The printed matter on that page was reset for inclusion in the main section with an explanation that something went awry. This was an enormous task. Dozens of people were brought in to rip out the offending page.

That is an example of the perils of the news biz. Naughty people out there try to trick us into doing awful and embarrassing things.

When I was working for the *Tribune* the paper bought an illustrated word-building feature for young readers. In about part four the feature said: "This is a truck. This is a duck. Can you think of any other words that end in -uck?" Well, the *Tribune* editors could think of one real quick, and that was the end of that little feature.

Also while at the *Tribune*, I met the guy who wrote the 1948 headline "Dewey Defeats Truman" in an election in which Truman won by 1.5 million votes. The hed writer's explanation: "The Colonel made me do it." The *Tribune* is still sensitive about that hed. A female reporter adorned her newsroom desk with that famous photo and an editor came over and told her "Get rid of that!"

Yeah, we make mistakes. One day at the *Journal* there was a report that a home on the south side had exploded. The *Journal* sent a reporter to investigate. The reporter called back about fifteen minutes later. "There is no such place," she said. "You must have the wrong address." The metro editor said that, well, we checked with police and fire and that was the address all right. The reporter said, "Well, I was over there and there's nothing there but a hole in the ground . . . " Yeah, that's the news biz. Sometimes we don't get it right and sometimes we don't get it, period.

When I was working for the *Sheboygan Press* I was doing a story about eleven blind people with seeing-eye dogs who were going to go through an obstacle course downtown to see how well master and dog performed together. I interviewed one of the participants, whose seeing-eye dog had bad breath, as I recall. I had one of these huge Speed Graphic cameras to take a picture of the two. I slapped a flashbulb in the nine-inch reflector, zeroed in and POW! snapped the picture. The seeing-eye dog began blinking madly. I later learned that this master and dog came in second to last in the contest. I really felt badly about that. (If you think that's funny, you are *sick*.)

One time a *Sentinel* photographer went out for evening lunch, had too many martinis and on his way back to work slammed into a police car. The cops swarmed over the guy's car and found a loaded revolver in the glove compartment. The photographer's co-workers were amused and puzzled. They said, "Lookit, we can understand your getting drunk. We can understand your getting into your car and driving drunk. We can understand your slamming into another car. We can understand that the car you chose to slam into was a police car. But what in the hell were you doing carrying a loaded revolver in your glove compartment?" The photographer replied: "Doesn't everybody?"

Gerald Kloss, one of the finest journalists I have ever encountered, wrote a humor column for The *Milwaukee Journal*'s Green Sheet called "Slightly Kloss-Eyed." He was extremely creative and incredibly funny. His poems would leave you in stitches.

During World War II Kloss served in the Army and was stationed at a base in Battle Creek, Michigan, where he worked on the base newspaper. One day Kloss encountered a German POW, late of Erwin Rommel's Afrika Korps, mopping floors in the infirmary. In what was perhaps his most notable contribution to the war effort, Sergeant Kloss taught this unfortunate POW (or fortunate, depending on your viewpoint) to sing "I'm Yust a Prizoner of Var" to the tune "Prisoner of Love."

Kloss continued such lyrical transpositions at *The Milwaukee Journal*. For the in-house paper, *The Little Journal*, Kloss wrote "Fight Song of the Company Man," to be sung to the tune "These Are Among My Favorite Things." Among the lyrics:

Smooth elevators
That never go fritz.
These are a few
Of our fringe benefits!

At farewell parties Kloss would provide hilarious, keepsake poems for the retiree, often managing to work the retiree's name into the rhyme. We always looked forward to these. If Kloss couldn't rhyme the last name, he would rhyme the first. And was he swift! One day he asked me, "Steve, what time is that retirement party?" I said "Five o'clock, at Turner's." Kloss said, "Well then I'd better get started on my poem." It was then two o'clock!

But Kloss, like Hank Aaron, could now and then strike out with the bases loaded. One day, for the Green Sheet, Kloss produced a Slightly Kloss-Eyed column delving into the problems of a mythical development he dubbed Auschwitz Acres. And I, as the copy editor. Well, what can I say? Even the great Gene Krupa once poked himself in the eye with a drumstick. I slapped together a punny hed for it: "Auschwitz Acres residents need some patio training."

Va-va-voom, Oy Vey, and Good Morning, Hiroshima! The place blew up. We wrote apologies for our lack of sensitivity and The Journal promised to take steps to make sure nothing like that ever happened again.

I got called into the office of managing editor-features. She was extremely upset. "Oh, this is terrible!" she exclaimed. "How could you DO such a thing! And now it looks like this is going to get over the wires and we are going to be embarrassed nationally. Oh, this is just awful!"

And I thought, well . . . it was indeed awful, a terrible blunder, but it wasn't the end of the world. After all, we are not *that* way. We apologized all over the place and now we should just let the thing pass over. Bad as it was, it certainly wasn't as awful as that Smothers Brothers thing: "On the third day, Christ rose from the dead, and, not seeing his shadow . . . "

So we apologized. "Mea culpa, mea culpa, mea *MAXIMA* culpa." Now what do you want us to do? Hurl ourselves into a cauldron of molten steel? Sure, we make blunders. Surprising we don't make more, considering how difficult and complicated it is putting out this thing we call "the daily miracle."

What about that obituary in which we buried the undertaker instead of the deceased? And what about that time *the Sentinel* ran a story in which it declared our retired chairman of the board dead before his number was up? (When you are trying to minimize the impact of your own gaffes it is always wise to cite blunders made by the competition!)

And what about that time we had to stop the presses because we had identified a rabbi as a rabbit? Yep, Forrest Gump had it right. Tish happens.

The Auschwitz Acres thing blew over in a week.

13

Ione

Ione Quinby Griggs was the *Journal*'s advice columnist. She was quite elderly, but she continued to produce a regular column for the Green Sheet. Ione would shuffle around the newsroom muttering "Ahem! Oh, boy" and stop at desk after desk to catch her balance as she waddled toward her own.

She had a few odd habits. She always wore a straw hat. Some believed this stemmed from the days when people would visit her in the newsroom and if she didn't want to talk to them she would say, "Well, I have to leave now," and since she had her straw hat on she looked ready for a trip.

She also kept her phone hidden in an upper desk drawer. When it would ring, she would open the drawer and grab the receiver. When done, she would hang up and close the drawer. So whenever we heard the muffled ring of a phone we knew Ione was getting another one. We didn't know where this habit came from. I thought it possibly stemmed from the days when there were not as many newsroom phones as journalists, and she made sure she had hers.

She had an enormous file of service agencies, and was effective at putting troubled callers in touch with those who could help them. However, I am afraid that Ione got taken in now and then by one of those naughty people. Like the item about the mean dairy farmer who would awaken his wife with a cattle prod and she would "hit the floor running." Nothing was beneath Ione. One day it was: "Yes, that's the Running Bare Nudist Colony. That's spelled B-A-R-E." Ione's voice resembled that of the wicked queen in "Snow White and the Seven Dwarfs," except it was higher pitched. She had a delightful sense of humor. I wish I had gotten to know her better. I never quite understood her; Dan Chabot, the Green Sheet editor, did.

Ione made the transition from typewriter to computer with little difficulty, although she regarded the computer as some sort of word-eating beast that would not let you have your words back once you put them in there. But she kept plugging away and writing her column.

Her age was the stuff of much speculation. I once tried my journalist's best to get her to reveal it. I asked, "Ione, when did you graduate from high school?" She went: "Ahem. Ahoom. Aham. Aheem. Ahim. Ahorm." (I didn't know there were than many ways to clear your throat.) For a while I thought I might have my answer. I did not. She finished "ahemming" and gave me a "Nice try, Sonny!" glare that was so piercing I believe I know what it's like to be on the business end of a flame-thrower.

Ione was a tough edit. Kept getting her "m's" and "n's" mixed up. Her advice tended to be a bit old-fashioned and often impractical, even trite. I herewith concoct a more or less typical item from IQG's column:

DEAR IQG: I am at wit's end. My husband ran off with the neighbor lady. My son is in jail on drug charges. My daughter has been arrested for shop-lifting. My dog bit a deliveryman and now he's suing. Yesterday I was fired from my job, and on the way home I hit a tree and totaled my car. What ever am I to do?—**CRUSHED**
DEAR CRUSHED: Count your blessings!

Ione was clearly feeling the ravages of age, and would have an "accident" or two in the office. Janine Ghelfi, a clerk typist in the Entertainment Department, watched over Ione, helping her around and making sure she got home all right. But the time was coming for Ione to give up her job. With reluctance, she retired in 1985 and entered a nursing home to get the special care she needed. We figured Ione's age to be eighty-four—certainly worth an entry in the *Guinness Book of World Records* as the world's oldest advice columnist.

At this time, a few of us got to visit her room at the Wisconsin Hotel on 3rd Street. It was like a peek inside King Tut's tomb. A bed with a white lace spread, table after little table filled with figurines, trinkets, doodads, knickknacks and faded pictures in gilded frames. Not a dreary place, but it was like stepping into another century.

When Ione entered the nursing home, certain official papers about her life had to be produced. It turned out that Ione, Keeper of Woman's Most Precious Secret, actually was ninty-four. She lived to be 100.

I am sure Ione left this earth with an "Ahem!"—and a wink.

14

Of Disappearing Vice Presidents

A Chicago journalist told me that a major Chicago bank let go a popular vice president with almost no explanation.

The journalist felt something fishy had happened. So on a hunch he called the bank president and said, "Is it true that Arthur Scheckels got the heave-ho because he stiffed your bank for three hundred thou?"

Bank president: (stunned silence) then, "How in the HELL did you find that ou . . . There's no truth to that statement whatsoever! Call public relations!"

Enterprising journalism. I love it.

Journal Communications Inc. once had a vice-president whom I will call Mr. Dour. He was a statistic-spewing know-it-all, and was as mirthless as a sack of dead rats. He arrived late to the company, having been brought in by the chairman of the board himself, and was considered to be on the fast track.

The Journal newsroom early in the year would hold its News Room Seminar, at which it would indulge in serious discussions about journalism. It followed the professional events with some levity. That year's seminar was held at a restaurant called Top of the First, on top of the then-First Wisconsin bank building. The Entertainment Department went out of its way to provide skits and humorous sketches for the evening. Some of the actors were staffers who were involved in local theater.

A few mukkymuks, including Mr. Dour, were invited to the event. Entertainment included singing by a metro desk secretary, Debbie Gilchrist, who had a marvelous voice. And there was a "Twilight Zone" spoof ("Doo-DOO-doo-doo") and a few other crazy things, all great fun.

The skit of the night was provided by Dominique Paul Noth, entertainment editor. He did a takeoff on the *Journal-Sentinel*'s Marketing Committee. He stood before his audience and, in a German accent, said, "Fierst ve must haff penetrashun!"—and he jabbed his right index finger menacingly across his chest. "Und zen, ve must haff zeerkulashun!" and he waggled his finger about, causing all those with prostrate problems to squirm uncomfortably.

It was great stuff. "Saturday Night Live" visits *The Milwaukee Journal*.

Mr. Dour was unamused. He thought the skit was tasteless and—horrors!—anti-Semitic. He demanded apologies all around, got them, and warned that in the future the newsroom would no longer be allowed to indulge in such insensitive levity. And from the Lifestyle Section on the south to the Sports Department on the north, a giant wet blanket descended upon *The Journal* newsroom. Our subsequent seminars were as exciting as nursing home knitting contests.

At one of those knitting contests, held at the Hyatt Regency, Mr. Dour himself was on the dais with Bob Wills, the *Sentinel*'s former Raging Bull and now a company vice president senior to Mr. Dour.

Journalists peppered the two veeps with questions about *The Journal*, the company, where are we going, how are we going to get there, etc. In response to one question, Mr. Dour replied, "Some day, when I run this place . . . " My eyes immediately shifted to Mr. Wills. I thought he reacted like a convicted murderer experiencing his first taste of hostile electricity in the Sing Sing electric chair. But then I have a florid imagination.

After the seminar, Mr. Dour's "Some day, when I run this place" remark became the talk of the newsroom. We were wondering how top management might react to it.

A few months later the news room was abuzz with something else. "It's Mr. Dour! He's gone! He's no longer here. He's vanished!"

It happened suddenly and without warning. Mr. Dour was no longer with the company. His name was stripped from the masthead and there was nothing to indicate what had happened, not even the usual "Mr. Dour has decided to pursue other career interests . . . " Nothing. These communications companies know how to create non-persons, I tell ya.

The sixth floor was stonewalling on the matter, and we journalists, however enterprising, were unable to find out exactly what happened.

And so, dear readers, by combining information, speculation, misinformation, and the worst -tion of all—imagination—I hereby construct a scenario of what possibly happened to Mr. Dour.

Mr. Dour's "Some day, when I run this place" remark truly upset Mr. Wills, and Mr. Wills wanted Mr. Dour out. But one vice president cannot fire another, so Mr. Wills needed allies. He discussed the matter with other vice presidents and company executives. They agreed that Mr. Dour was a problem, that his high-handedness was most upsetting and they agreed that Mr. Dour had gone too far and felt that it was time for Mr. Dour to take a trip. Mr. Wills lined up as many allies as he could, then presented the matter to the chairman of the board, who had brought Mr. Dour aboard in the first place.

The chairman, confronted with this mass of non-support for Mr. Dour, agreed that it was time to get rid of Mr. Dour. But he told Mr. Wills, "I don't want anything to do with it. You take care of it." Mr. Wills said he would.

So one day Mr. Wills summoned Mr. Dour into his office. As soon as Mr. Dour was safely inside, Mr. Wills leaned over to the right side of his desk and pushed a red button. A trap door opened, Mr. Dour fell through, Building Services was called to suture the hole in the floor, and Mr. Dour—like the man in the folk song from the 1960s who boarded a Boston subway train and was never heard from again—became "The Man Who Never Returned."

However, unlike that unfortunate subway passenger, "whose fate is still unlearned," some news surfaced about Mr. Dour. He attempted to get a job with another communications company. Unfortunately for Mr. Dour, an executive with that company had once worked for Journal Communications and had had a most unpleasant clash with Mr. Dour. This executive got on the horn and managed to put the kabosh on the hire.

Ah so! As Confucius might say: "Man you kick in gonads today become man who kick YOU in gonads to-morry!"

15

Interns, Gifts, Seminars

Every summer the *Journal* would bring into the news room eight to twelve interns, seniors, juniors and sometimes sophomores in college, to give them some hands-on journalism experience and to fill in for staffers on vacation.

I once asked Pat Graham, at the time in charge of interns, "How long does it take to find out whether an intern has the stuff to make a journalist?" Graham's reply: "Two to three weeks." Yup! By their first endeavors ye shall know them.

Most of our interns came from Marquette University or the University of Wisconsin-Milwaukee. The question was often raised: Who were better, the Marquette interns or the UWM interns? Answer: The Marquette interns were better writers, the UWM interns had more hustle. But UWM produced Bill Jones, a managing editor for the *Chicago Tribune*, and Marquette did not, so na-na-na-na-NAH-na.

Our youngest intern ever was a lively young lady from Philadelphia, Bernadine Waller. She was related to the jazz pianist/singer Fats Waller ("Ain't Misbehavin'," "Your Feets Too Big.") Her presence was like having a young Pearl Bailey in the news room. She thought I looked like the actor Walter Matthau, and I tried not to disappoint. I would help her start the day by taking a Matthau-like line from "The Odd Couple" and say, "You're driving me crazy, Bernadine!" and she would shriek in delight. When Bernadine's birthday arrived, staffer Georgia Pabst organized a newsroom party for her.

The very good interns—and about a third of them fit this category—were a great source of new hires. But, alas, the lower third were—not so good.

It's difficult to imagine this nowadays, but there was a time when it was routine for journalists to accept gifts from news sources and others trying to curry favor with the media. Around Christmastime journalists' desks would be littered with goodies—crystal figurines, ashtrays, bottles of booze, calendars, notebooks, leather folders, hams, turkeys, boxes of candy, nuts . . . I still possess a patent leather folder I got from a news source while working for the *Tribune.*

At Christmastime in Milwaukee the Miller Brewing Company and now defunct Jos. Schlitz Brewing Company would send cases of beer to staff members of *The Milwaukee Journal* and *Sentinel.* I got home from work one day to find my case of Schlitz outside my apartment door—absent one six-pack snitched by another dweller who felt that three six-packs was enough for a journalist. I didn't make any quid-pro-quo connection to such gifts. And anyway, my favorite beer was Pabst.

Ron Leys, then a copy editor on Local Desk, so appreciated his gift of beer that he sent a case of his own basement-brewed stuff to the president of Schlitz. He received a warm thank-you note.

This gifts-for-journalists practice was global. When I was working for the *Herald* in Australia I was in a butcher shop for something or other, I cannot remember what. Perhaps I was doing a story about a retiring butcher that was destined to bear the *Herald* headline "Goodbye, Mr. Chops" or something. Anyway, I was talking to this butcher and he grabs a piece of butcher paper, wraps a bunch of sausages and sliced meat in it and hands it to me. I accepted it without qualms. Sort of like a tip for the chronically underpaid. But even as Richard Nixon would say, "That would be wrong!" And indeed, it was the Watergate scandal that brought a halt to boodle in the newsroom.

In 1973 the *Journal* hauled a bunch of us down to a room on the third floor to discuss the question of journalists accepting gifts. The editors already had decided they would tell Schlitz and Miller to stop sending free beer to our journalists. I was totally in favor of the beer ban. But then the matter turned to prize money for Milwaukee Press Club awards. Winners would receive $50 taken from donations to the Press Club from Wisconsin businesses.

I said that the award-winners should be allowed to accept this prize money. "All that is happening," I argued, "is that Wisconsin and Milwaukee businesses are showing their support for the Milwaukee Press Club. And some of this 'support' is used as prizes for Milwaukee Press Club award winners. What's wrong with that? By the time the award-winners get the money it has been sufficiently laundered . . . so . . . that . . . " And that was the end of prize money for Press Club contest winners. Damn! A $700 mistake!

And so the boodle era ended. Gifts continued to arrive in the newsroom, but staffers were told they could not keep them, and they didn't. I thought Jerry Kloss, our poet laureate and lyricist, might come up with something to note the end of the boodle era. For instance, he could have written some lyrics to be sung to "I've Got the Sun in the Morning and the Moon at Night":

No more Miller's
No more Schlitz
The Journal newsroom
Has become the pits.

But perhaps certain situations do not lend themselves well to such levity.

Every now and then the *Journal* would bring in journalists to conduct seminars for writers and copy editors. One such seminar was given by a Mr. Bremner, an Australian who was a shirt-tail relative of *Journal* writer Margo Bremner Huston, the *Journal*'s last Pulitzer Prize winner.

At the Bremner seminar, the subject of obscenities came up. It was the 1970s, and the spoiled, "Howdy-Doody"-weaned Baby Boomers were throwing another one of their collective temper tantrums. How do we deal with the avalanche of obscenities? Use dashes to substitute for the offending words? Edit around the offending words and don't refer to them at all? What? I argued vociferously against using dashes. "It's like running a crossword puzzle for idiots," I said. "Anybody can figure out what the f—ing dashes mean." My suggestion: Run the offending words—but spell them backwards. The reaction to this suggestion was what I would call bemused befuddlement. In the end I could tell they thought it a perfectly tishy idea.

We had two excellent editing seminars run by Buck Ryan of the *Chicago Tribune*. At one of them Ryan told us of the *Pocatello* (Idaho) *Tribune* winning the "tasteless headline of the year" award. The headline, on a story about an all-gay rodeo: "Homo on the range." Lookit. I'm neither gay nor homophobic, but THAT'S a good hed, and I would definitely run it if I were editor. Which is perhaps why I never became an editor.

16

Adios

People would leave the *Journal* various ways. Some would quit for a job elsewhere and leave without fanfare. Some would leave or retire and have a huge farewell party that included a keepsake poem by the *Journal*'s poet laureate, Jerry Kloss. Some would quit in disgust, some would be forced out, some would be fired.

We once had a part-time writer whose work the editors did not like at all, so she was terminated. But the writer was not going to take this snub quietly. On her final day she marched down Editors' Row, pounding on each door and screaming her frustrations at the occupants inside. Then she stormed into an elevator and left. Wow! What chutzpah! What style!

There was a story here, of course, if newspapers would cover stories about their newsrooms, which they don't. And, of course, I have a hed for it: "Angry retiree gives editors both barrels." (Good hed, too. You can run it one column, two column or spread) But, nah. All we got was a notice on the bulletin board: "Sylvia Schluggermuck has left *The Journal* to pursue other career interests."

Some people retired quietly and without retirement parties. Retiree Jack Letellier slinked out of the place without signing off his computer. This is a very dangerous thing to do. Other journalists could send angry messages out under Letellier's name. In fact, such shenanigans were not uncommon in that newsroom. Neil Rosenberg became a regular office menace pitting staffers against each other by sending insulting memos over their untended machines.

Some people got passed over for promotion and left in disgust. One was Dick Pufall, heir-apparent to become sports editor until the editor had other ideas. Dick left in disgust. He returned a few years ago to the *Journal Sentinel* and is one of the reasons the sports section has the best headlines in the paper.

Michelle Thompson was another. She had filled in, quite capably, as editor of the Lifestyle and Business sections, and was well-liked by the staff. But for some reason or another, the *Journal* wouldn't give her an editorship, so she left for the *Atlanta Journal*, and word quickly spread north that she was managing a larger group of people than she ever had in Milwaukee. One could almost hear the na-na-na-na-NAH-nah roaring up I-75.

Gerald Kloss said that at one farewell party, the retiree, overcome by the sendoff, decided at the last second not to leave. "And the S.O.B. kept the farewell gifts, too," Kloss said.

Then there was the writer who had fifteen farewell parties and never attended any of them. That was Ed Williams, the aviation writer. Ed left in 1972, partyless. The annual Ed Williams Party was the brainchild of Doug Armstrong, one of the most talented—certainly the most versatile—members of the staff.

Armstrong was, variously, automotive writer, film critic, financial writer. He covered anything, and did a superb job.

Armstrong said the idea of the Ed Williams farewell party came when the *Journal* was losing staffers to other papers. Armstrong thought it would be a good idea to throw a party for someone who stayed. But then it was revealed that Ed Williams left without benefit of a party, so Armstrong and friends decided maybe they should throw an annual party for Ed.

Promotion of the party was imaginative and hilarious. An 8½ by 11 sheet of paper would appear on the staff bulletin board. In the center was a tiny picture of Ed. Each day the picture got larger and larger. It's coming! The Ed Williams farewell party!

The party was usually held at The Harp, a bar along the Milwaukee River. At one party Armstrong stood up and, wearing a World War II aviator's cap, delivered "An Ode to the F-4F," or some other piece of nonsense.

Armstrong also was the *Journal*'s Steven Spielberg, producing films about the newsroom that had us all in stitches. In one of those films, the plot, if you want to call it that, involved a reporter, played by staffer Alan Borsuk, who witnessed an ax murder at a meeting of the Southeastern Wisconsin Regional Planning Commission (SEWRPAC). But "nothing ever happens" at SEWRPAC meetings, so the editors refused to buy Borsuk's tale. Borsuk tried desperately to sell the story to other editors, including sports editor Chuck Johnson. But all Johnson wanted to know was "Who won?" At film's end Borsuk was shown driving north to Sheboygan, apparently to try to sell the story to the *Sheboygan Press*. The film starred Harry Hill, assistant managing editor, shown lying on his desk reading a feelthy magazine; metro editor Patrick Graham hopping around in a Superman costume, and various staffers at work, including Ione Quinby Griggs tapping away at her computer.

The Ed Williams party filled the staffers' need for mirth after Mr. Dour destroyed the frivolity they had enjoyed at the news seminars. Since this was a private party,

the mukkymuks could do nothing about it. The party included gag gifts, a whole lot of political incorrectness and
the merciless ribbing of staffers, management and news
makers.

17

News Judgment

Newspapers have a nasty habit of copying one another. When *USA Today* debuted in the early 1980s with its TV-era design and colored logos it wasn't but a few months before newspapers across America began to mimic the makeup (including—horrors!—the *Chicago Tribune*).

This national aping was followed by a severe decline in newspaper subscribership, which publishers blamed on everything but their copycat policies. I am convinced that it is newspapers' tendency to goose-step with one another that is behind the decline in circulation. What happens when Baskin & Robbins cuts its flavors from thirty-five to thirty-one? The devotees of the four dropped flavors might settle on other flavors—or they might stop eating ice cream altogether. When newspapers throw away the most important thing they have—their distinctive looks and personalities—they hand readers a gold-plated invitation to dump them.

Then there is the Blood/Chaos/Politics Syndrome, which drives almost all newspapers and some other media as well. The bloodier a story is, the more chaotic it is, the more political it is, the more likely it will find preferred space in the paper. The losers: Humor and pathos for two.

Some day, read your newspaper with a pen in hand. If you see a positive story, mark it with a +. If you see a negative story, mark it with a −. If the story is neutral, give it a =. When you are done you are going to find

yourself swimming in a sea of —s. The BCP Syndrome is
alive and well in America's newspapers.

And yet the wonderful stories are there. They just get
shunted aside by the BCP Syndrome. Wonderful stories
make the paper, sure. Page 3, four inches, 18 point hed.
But the man who murders and cannibalizes his granny
gets page one, 40 inches and a 48-point hed.

I offer three examples of news stories that I felt were
underplayed or misplayed in the *Journal* and *Journal Sentinel* over the years. I thought all three were page oners.

Story One: Lone passenger boards a plane for a non-
stop flight from Kuwait to London. He gets to London.
Something's wrong. What happened? The airline lost his
luggage. I think this would make a hilarious story out
front with the headline: "Well . . . ANYBODY can make
a mistake!"

Story Two: English girl, age fourteen, flies to Spain
with mommy and favorite auntie to attend a music festi-
val. On way back plane crashes and burns. Mommy and
auntie die in the flames, girl is injured and taken to a
hospital. When girl is told her mommy and auntie are
dead, she closes her eyes, falls back on her bed and shuts
herself off from the world. Hospital staff can do nothing
to bring her out of this self-induced trance. Then someone
has an idea. Next day Princess Diana visits the hospital.
She sits on girl's bed and talks to her. Girl opens her eyes,
sits up, starts to cry. Diana hugs her and brings her back
into this world. Ho-hum. Four inches, Page 3, 18 point
hed. Again, this one could have been run out front with
the hed: "The touch of a princess." There's even a "Sleeping Beauty" allegory here. I wrote an angry memo to an
editor about that one.

Story Three: In February 2002 the *Journal Sentinel* ran a story about some guy from Texas who goes flippo every time he hears certain words, among them "Wisconsin." I know that newspapers are leery about they're-coming-to-take-me-away-ha-ha types, but I felt that a story about a guy who goes nuts at the mention of Wisconsin ought to get better play in a newspaper in Wisconsin. Possible headline: "Un-Wisconsin." (Or turn the hed over to some really good hed writer, like Becky Williams or Frank Clines.)

So it's not that the nice stories aren't there. It's that the mirthful and touching stories are continually buried under an avalanche of BCPs. We seem terrified to make readers laugh or cry, but seem to get perverse glee in making them feel depressed.

Some papers, like the old *Milwaukee Sentinel*, tried to give readers some dessert with their meal of BCP. The *Sentinel* featured Super Writer Bill Janz out front. Janz had a wonderful touch, and could make almost any story interesting. He was like an oasis in that paper, and his column was always among the first things I read.

If you bought newspapers from around the country and spread them before you you would notice their remarkable similarity—not in the stories they offer, but in their slavish adherence to the BCP Syndrome. The Green Sheets have been killed off because they're considered old-fashioned—or perhaps it's because editors think that humor and pathos are old-fashioned. Yet, newspaper circulation continues to plummet, and I am personally convinced that the BCP Syndrome is responsible. We are just t-o-o serious. And I can't remember when I read a truly funny story in the paper.

When people think of newsrooms and news judgment they probably conjure up the scene from the movie "All the President's Men," where a gaggle of editors meet with the managing editor to assess what stories the readers should be presented that day. We get the impression that the stuff in America's newspapers is the product of the contemplation of wizened (sometimes), male (predominantly), elderly (often), sober (most of the time) professorial types (occasionally) who combine their journalistic expertise and experience to determine what the readers ought to know. And that is true—sometimes.

When I worked for the *Tribune*, I had the delight of sitting in for the foreign editor when he took off for dinner after the first edition came out at about 5 P.M. The *Tribune* senior editors sat at desks on two raised platforms in the center of the newsroom. These desks were occupied by the editor-in-chief, managing editor, news editor, national editor, state editor and makeup editor. The eight editors (including me) would flip through the *Tribunes* as they came off the presses. They often acted as though they knew exactly what was in the paper.

Then copies of the rival *Sun-Times* were wheeled in and distributed to the various editors and the fun began. The editors would check those *Sun-Times*es like garment inspectors looking for faulty stitching in batches of aprons. Then there would be a scream: "Why didn't we have this?" and the sound of paper being torn and a reporter rushing to get the clip and do a story on the information. Or "Charlie, make sure we have this for the second edition." Or, "Omigod! Look at Page five!" One editor got so excited about an error he found in the *Sun-Times* that he tore out the page, marked it for correction and sent it to the *Tribune* composing room. Such things would drive the *Tribune* printers out of their tree.

Al Gray, a police reporter at the *Tribune*, told me of the day he had a story of the Coast Guard heading out into Lake Michigan to extinguish a fire on a boat and then towing the boat and the couple aboard back to port. He asked the city editor how much copy he wanted. The city editor held his left hand aloft and with his thumb and index finger signaled, four, perhaps three inches.

Gray did the story, which appeared on about page 17 with a one-column hed. The *Sun-Times*, meanwhile, played the story on page 3 with a spread hed: "Prominent couple rescued from burning boat." Al said the city editor told him to goose up the story, and for the second edition the Tribune ran it—not to get *too* excited here—with a three column hed on page 5. Meanwhile, the *Sun-Times* saw how the *Trib* had played the story, so it trimmed it, put a smaller hed on it and shoved it back to about page 10.

So, yes, news judgment often is the product of wizened, elderly, sober, professorial journalists pooling their expertise and experience to bring its readers what they think they ought to know. And other times, news judgment is more like a toy fight in a day-care center.

18

Crisis

In June 1985 what I call the Napoleon Regime took over. I call it that because of something I read years later in a book, *The Inner Game of Management.* (See Chapter 5, "The Napoleon Syndrome.")

Out was the warm, outgoing Editor-in-Chief Dick Leonard, who would routinely show up at farewell parties for staffers. (He also was an avid horseman. One day he took his steed from a stable south of Port Washington and galloped into that town, tying his animal to a post in front of the Smith Bros. Restaurant.) After retirement, Leonard became a professor of journalism at Marquette University.

Out also was Joe Shoquist, managing editor, who hired me in 1969 (thanks, Joe). Joe would become dean of the University of South Carolina journalism school, and have the same impact on that school that Lou Holtz later had on the South Carolina football team.

George Lockwood, managing editor-features, left a bit later to become a journalism professor at Marshall University in West Virginia. He told me he felt he didn't fit in with the new team. Lockwood helped me in my move to the Entertainment Department. He was my guardian angel. His departure would create a crisis for me later.

Harry Hill, the personable assistant managing editor, had the unmitigated gall to die of a stroke on March 7, 1984. Hill loved children, and at parties he would let staffers' kiddies crawl all over him.

The Napoleon Regime's editor-in-chief came from the thumb-sucking, navel-contemplating world of the editorial writer, rather than from the smash-mouth, trench-warfare world of the newsroom. That's not necessarily bad in itself. But there were other troubling factors in his leadership, among them his messianic personality, his preoccupation with minutiae, his lack of people skills, and his ignorance of day-to-day news operations.

The new managing editor was one of the finest writers ever to grace the pages of the paper, but he had spent little time in the newsroom and lacked rapport with staff.

Napoleon and Company also brought with it a brutal but perhaps not unusual management style. Editors would sit in their offices and shove journalists around boards like so many chess pieces. Then it was "Fix bayonets!" and they would force the screaming wretches into their new positions. I dubbed this the Bataan Death March-style of management, and I became one of the screaming wretches.

At this time I was probably the happiest member of the *Journal* staff. I was the copy editor for the Green Sheet and entertainment section, a job I had my eyes on almost from the day I set foot in the *Journal*. It took a long time to get there. I worked the Local and National desks for eleven years, also filling in as needed at the State Desk, Sports and Picture Desk (lots). I was a regular Suitcase Simpson. It was handy for the *Journal*, because the paper didn't have great copy-editing depth. But it got tiring, and I yearned one day to have a "home" in the newsroom.

Half the time I didn't know what desk to report to, which could result in hilarious situations. One day John Rammel, the picture editor, scheduled me to work the picture desk. Ruth Wilson, meanwhile, had scheduled me to work the Local Copy Desk. I showed up for work and sat down at the picture desk. Ruth came over to complain that I was supposed to be working the local desk. Rammel was on his feet screaming that I was his for the day. The two went at it, yelling and unyielding.

They finally reached a compromise: I would work the picture desk for the first edition, then rush over to the local desk, which had a later deadline for the first edition. Then I would rush back to the picture desk to work the latest edition, then rush back to the local desk to edit stuff there—sometimes getting back just in time to edit photo captions I had just written on the picture desk. It was a crazy day, not without laughs. But I was tiring of this sort of thing.

From time to time, Jerry Wilkerson, editor of the Home Section, would borrow me to edit stories for his section. In 1981, when there was an opening on the Home Section, he urged me to apply for it. And that year I left the confines of the day-to-day deadline desks and moved to the Home Section. I got to do some writing also, and thoroughly enjoyed that. I also got to work with a pair of office comics, Dennis Getto and Jerry Van Ryzin. When Wilkerson, a wonderful boss, left for a job in Texas he was replaced by Eleanor Coleman, another superb boss.

Lockwood was well aware of my desire to get to the Entertainment Department. So when Ben Waxse, the copy editor handling the Green Sheet, retired, I thought my day had arrived. But no. Jackie Loohauis, an excellent writer with a light touch, was working part-time for Entertainment. They wanted to hire her full time. I could hardly argue with that. So I waited about a year, and in March 1983, when there was a transfer involving the Lifestyle Section and Entertainment, I got my big break and became copy editor of the Green Sheet and various sections in

Entertainment. I was on top of the world. But the powers that be had other ideas.

One day in February 1987 I was asked to report to the office of the deputy managing editor. I had no idea what for. I entered his office. He opened the conversation, "As a valued employee, you . . ." Hold it, hold it, hold it right there. All right, all you peons, slaves of industry, unappreciated workers, time-clock punchers, nine-to-fivers, underpaid grunts, and you, Mrs. Calabash (wherever you are). When you are called into an office and the boss opens the conversation with "As a valued employee . . ." look out. Something dreadful might happen. I understand that the last words Marie Antoinette heard on this earth were: "As a valued member of the French monarchy . . . ka-chung!"

Back to the deputy's office.

"As a valued *Journal* employee, you are being sent to the local copy desk. You have no choice in this matter. So please stop squirming, as I do not wish for you to sully the blade of my bayonet."

Ka-chung! Just like that—except for the bayonet part. I was being sent back to the last place in the newsroom I ever wanted to see again (if anybody had bothered to ask, which, of course, they didn't) and I had no say in the matter. I know that journalists are supposed to go where they are needed, but I felt I had paid my dues big time and had earned the right to a say in my fate. I also knew that this transfer would never be made if I hadn't lost my guardian angel.

I was shocked. And furious. And I felt cheated. And frustrated. I could find no compelling reason for their making this move, and none was ever explained to me. I was getting very good performance reviews and I was getting along with everybody. I will admit that I was never a candidate for a managerial goody-two-shoes award, but I wasn't *that* bad.

I decided to fight this transfer. So I did what we journalists tell readers to do when they call to gripe about something in the paper. I wrote a letter to the editor! I was granted an interview, although "audience" might be a more accurate description of it.

I entered the editor's office at the appropriate time. The managing editor was there, sitting on a stool at one of the small round tables in the office. I took a stool to his right.

Then the editor made his appearance. He had his arms crossed, his hands cupping his shoulders. From about twelve feet back he took a step forward and swayed to his right: "I AM THE EDITOR of one of the last major evening newspapers in the United States," he declared. Then he took another step slightly to his left: "I AM entrusted with making The *Milwaukee Journal* a successful and relevant newspaper." Then he veered to the right: "I AM going to bring the *Journal* back to its days of greatness . . ."

I did not know what to make of this. I looked at the managing editor. He was plainly embarrassed, and wouldn't return my glance. I thought: An editor is not supposed to act like this! An editor is supposed to sit there with his feet on his desk, like Jason Robards, and he's supposed to say something like "What's your problem, kid?"

But this? I wondered where I had seen such a performance before. Sure! On *The Honeymooners*. Jackie Gleason, as Ralph Kramden, strutting around his apartment yelling, "Just remember, Alice. I'M THE KING! And you're nuthin', nuthin'." I am sure that's the message the editor was trying to send to me. The only message I got was that this guy had rocks in his head.

The discussion got nowhere. All the editor would say was "The needs of the *Journal* dictate . . . " And I will never forget the look of disdain the editor gave me, like "Why do I have to waste my time on a small matter like this when I have more important things to do?"

Well, dear readers, mistreated peons, unthanked laborers, nine-to-fivers (especially the wrong way), Mr. and Mrs. America and all the ships at sea, time-clock punchers, underpaid workers, and you, Mrs. Calabash (wherever you are). If I had been the Man of Courage, upon hearing "The needs of the *Journal* dictate . . . " for the umpteenth time, I should have said, "Well, the needs of Steve Maersch dictate otherwise. Get yourself another copy editor." And walked out. But I was the Chicken Man, so I grabbed my rifle and meekly headed back to the front.

Anyway, I could not walk out. I wasn't even close to being financially independent, I was forty-nine, which is not a good age for a journalist to go job-hunting. It also is an age when managers know they can slam the screws to you. I was still single, but destined later that year to marry a wonderful girl named Judy, the first girl I had ever fallen in love with, thirty-one years before, when she was fourteen and I eighteen.

I left the editor's office feeling more wretched than ever. I had tried to save a job I had worked so hard and long to get, and I could not do it. Some might argue, Maersch, why didn't you just report to the local copy desk and give it your best shot? Simple: I did not want to become a dispirited hulk working at a desk I wanted nothing to do with and nursing a groin wound until I could take early retirement in six years and get the hell out of there. I wanted to be happy in my work.

As the day approached when I would have to report to the dreaded local copy desk I grew more and more depressed. Then I thought, come on, Maersch, don't let them get away with this. I sent a letter to the deputy managing editor saying this whole job transfer thing had left me wretchedly depressed, that I didn't think it was fair to treat me this way considering what I had done for the company. I said I wanted to work here, but I was tired of being kicked around the newsroom like this, and I wanted it to stop (I was hinting at a contract of some sort). I said I wanted to continue working in the Entertainment Department and if they couldn't let me do that, well, then fire me and get it over with. And I promised plenty of fireworks if they did that.

Well, they didn't fire me. They let me stay in Entertainment. In fact, I thought they backed off rather sheepishly. But I had groveled, and I am not proud of that.

I sent thank-yous to all the editors involved, although I had completely lost respect for them for the way they handled this and I certainly didn't trust them.

I later learned that the managing editor-features had asked an editor in entertainment how I would react to being transferred to the local copy desk. This editor said I probably would be very angry at first, but then would go along with it. Wonderful! I'm the guy being transferred and some other guy gets to do my job interview for me.

I came away from this incident with a view of managing people. A "valued employee" should be treated with more consideration than a new hire.

When the smoke cleared from this battle, I was paid a visit by Tom Barber, now news editor. He was angry. "I wish you would stop referring to the local copy desk as 'the Eastern Front,' " he said. "We're trying to get people to work over there."

Well . . . No one from management poked any sticks in my cage in my remaining eight years at the *Journal*. I won the headline award four more times, pulled out one year because I was beginning to feel like a pig, and won the Harry Hill Award for copy editing, my proudest achievement.

I was hardly the only person to have a run-in with the Napoleon Regime. This heavy-handed treatment of staffers continued, and staff morale suffered.

Some time after this I was elected to the Unitholders (stockholders) Council, which represented the peons concerns to management. As a result, I got to serve a year as a guest member of the Board of Directors. "Guest" means you sit there like Lot's wife and take in the proceedings; you don't try to offer suggestions on how to run the company, as one guest unitholder member did.

It was interesting observing the managers of the subsidiaries explain how their operations were faring. And it gave me a new view of this thing called "spin." But I concluded that Journal Communications and its subsidiaries were, for the most part, in good hands.

At a board meeting on one wintry day the chairman of the board, Tom McCollow, complained, "I didn't get a *Journal* delivered to my home last night. What could have gone wrong?" The circulation manager sat there in silence. Fortnight later—ta-da!—a new circulation manager.

As late as 1967, daily *Journal* circulation was more than 374,000. It then began a gradual but relentless slide. By 1985, when Napoleon and Company took over, circulation was about 295,000.

When a newspaper is losing circulation, there is an effort to find out why. The Napoleon Regime seemed to think a major problem was the design. I frankly liked the design of the paper at this time—attractive logos, easy-to-read type faces, simple and direct headlines. Readers often regard their newspaper as an institution, something they can count on in an uncertain world. So a massive redesign can be risky, like painting Gesu Church purple.

The Napoleon Regime decided the paper needed a major overhaul. So a gaggle of journalists and designers, working in a farmhouse in Pennsylvania (of all places) set out to design a paper to be marketed in Milwaukee, Wisconsin.

What they came back with looked like the result of a desk-clearing brawl in a typography factory that had merged with a wallpaper company. Every typographical gimmick known to man was incorporated into this design. There were eyebrows and ribbons and box quotes and pods, and icons and thumbnails and kickers and nods. The paper began to look like a junkyard.

The design came with impossible instructions. News heds were to be set flush left, feature heds were to be centered. What, then, do we do with news-features? No one knew. Headlines were allotted kickers (overlines) as well as decks. What was to be the function of the kicker? Was it to be a classifying tag to be used by people who read papers that way? If so, a story about Iran would logically have the kicker "Iran." But what if the hed writer wanted to start his main hed with the word Iran? Then he would have an "Iran" and "Iran" stacked together. Don't want that. So he would put something else in the kicker. This brought inconsistency into the world of kickers.

Then some hed writers would use the kickers as life rafts for information that should have been contained in the main hed. There were too many typographical gimmicks available and no rules to determine when and where they should be used. The paper began to look as though it were being produced by groups of committees that didn't talk to one another. It was a case of overcommunication breeding confusion and ultimately incoherence.

The readers hated the new design. The newsroom phones rang angrily for weeks after its introduction. Then the angry calls tapered off and the cancellations began pouring in.

We had painted Gesu Church purple.

19

Management

A newsroom is like a day-care center for egomaniacs, tough to manage. I suppose the best way to manage one is to put the round pegs in the round holes and the square pegs in the square holes, and then, if they're doing their jobs properly, let them alone. This still leaves you with the nuts, dolts, flakes, drunks, drug addicts, slobs, back-biters, snipers, malingerers, cheats and downright dangerous people. We even had a murderer in our newsroom, although he wasn't a journalist. He was a newsroom messenger. Killed a nice girl who worked in the news library.

I don't believe that an editor need be a journalist. I think it would suffice for her to know the product and know how to handle people. I think Lee Iacocca of Chrysler Corporation or Jack Welch of General Electric would have been excellent editors. Douglas MacArthur and George S. Patton would have been disasters—as would Napoleon. I've never managed people, but I think a secret to managing them is that they are people, not machines. They have spirits. I believe that one of the failures of the Napoleon regime was its inability to recognize people as spirits. To them they were mere machines in a journalism factory. Need a copy editing machine on the local copy desk? Simple. Unbolt a copy editing machine from the Entertainment Department, wheel it across the floor, plug it in and it soon will be happily chirping away. Hah!

Every two or so years we staffers would get questionnaires to fill out about our career status. We would get such questions as "How do you like your job?" "What can we do to make it better?" "Where do you hope to be five years from now?" etc. We would fill out these forms with great care. It was our career, you know. In actuality, this ritual reminded me of the cowboys playing the harmonica at night to keep the steers from stampeding. The managers could do whatever they wanted to do with us, and the cowboys were tricking their herds into marching to the slaughterhouse.

Most editors are chosen by the company's board of directors or specific members of the board. I believe a news organization could become more efficient if it allowed the journalists to have input in choosing the editor. At least advisory input. A vote of confidence. Might save a lot of trouble later on.

Journalists are terribly contrary and independent people. You tell them to do one thing, and they will do precisely the opposite. But, then, they are hired to be independent thinkers whose role in this world is to ferret out the BS—except that generated in their own newsrooms, of course.

One day a mouse got into our newsroom, probably making its way from the cafeteria, which was on the same floor as the newsroom. This is when I discovered that it is not only women who go "EEEEEEK!" The managing editor put a notice on the bulletin board stating that we had a "rodent problem" in the newsroom and we should be careful about bringing food in there. One day I bought bag of peanuts from the fourth floor confections machine. I stopped at the desk of Ron Leys, fellow member of the Sheboygan Mafia, and offered him some. I shook some peanuts into Ron's right hand. He transferred a few peanuts to his left hand and threw them on the floor for the office mouse.

Journalists are like that. Contrary. Independent. Cynical. But then, isn't that what they're hired for?

The *Journal* news room became unionized in 1982. I didn't favor a union. It meant that now we had to worry about two bosses instead of the devil we knew. The *Chicago Tribune* didn't have a union when I was there and still doesn't. There was absolutely no sentiment for a union at the *Tribune* when I worked there, and it had nothing to do with a company effort to keep one out. The employees kept the union out, and I think they did so because they were happy with the way their bosses treated them. I certainly was. And money is hardly the only reason why people seek the cover of unions.

Let's say the *Tribune* pays its 700 journalists $1,000 a week while the rival *Sun-Times* pays its 700 journalists $1,100 a week. I doubt the pay figures are right, but the difference between them probably is. A *Tribune* journalist is not likely to leap across the street to get the extra $100 a week only to see a big chunk of it go to higher taxes and union dues (which are not cheap) and lose all seniority perks in the bargain. What's the difference between paying 700 journalists $1,000 a week and 700 journalists $1,100 a week? It's a cool $3.8 million. Out of this, the *Tribune* could take $0.8 million to feather the nests of its journalists with 401K plans and things like that, making it even less likely that they'll jump ship. The *Tribune* gets the advantages, including a grip on quality control. Unions have a dreadful habit of defending incompetent workers as well as getting into petty turf wars with management that hurt the workers as well as the company.

I don't recall any worker being fired in my almost four years at the *Trib*, although there must have been a case or two. We used to get our raises in the spring. If the editors were not satisfied with a journalist's performance they would freeze him—that is, no raise. The journalists would get the message and leave.

I believe a lot of this started with Colonel Robert R. McCormick. The Colonel actually was three people. He was a right-wing opinionist, a man, as some said, "with the best mind of the 14th century." (Twelfth century is more like it.) And he used his newspapers as much as political organs as journalistic enterprises. True, and truly awful, and this led to the creation of the *Chicago Sun* in 1944 (it later merged with the *Times*). The Colonel also was an astute businessman, always employing the latest equipment and techniques. The third Colonel was the paternalistic boss. Since he hated unions—or any other bureaucracies that interfered with his running of his company—he would do whatever was necessary to keep unions out of his company. That meant treating his workers fairly and with respect.

During World War II he promised all *Tribune* employees who went off to war that they would get their jobs back when they returned. The Colonel subsidized the military pay of many of these workers to help their families back home. Such practices resulted in extreme loyalty to the Colonel, even from those who couldn't agree with him politically.

When he neared death in 1955, the Colonel was asked how long his *Tribune* would continue to be the flag-waving bastion of conservative political thought that he had made it. He guessed 15 years. Prescient thinking. In 1969 Clayton Kirkpatrick took the helm of the *Tribune*, and while the paper continued to be editorially conservative it also became wonderfully open and certainly is one of America's finest newspapers.

20

The End

By the end of 1992, *Journal* circulation had tumbled to 241,000 (*Sentinel* circulation was 169,000) and the Uppers decided it was time for Napoleon to take a trip.

In his farewell story, the editor, far from admitting to any mistakes, patted himself on the back and described his career at the *Journal* as one long parade of successes, culminating with his marvelous stewardship of the newspaper, and weren't we all fortunate to be the benefactors of such brilliant work.

And now, still in his fifties, he was retiring, leaving us with this joyous legacy and going off to conquer other journalistic worlds (or perhaps to get a job writing prospectuses for Enron Corp). A reader who didn't know better could easily conclude that The *Journal* was parting with the greatest editor it ever had. I got sick reading this.

Did anything go wrong? Any mistakes made? Any regrets? No way. This was an American Success Story. Actually, it was like Capt. E.J. Smith painting "Have a nice day" on the *Titanic* after it had hit the berg.

The facts: Under Napoleon, the *Journal* lost almost 60,000 subscribers (20 percent), the worst performance of any editor in the paper's history. Newsroom morale was like that of an NFL team looking at a 3 and 13 season. And anyone who now thought the *Journal* had a chance of surviving was capable of incredible self-delusion.

The staff hardly shared Napoleon's assessment of himself. One long-time mid-level editor called him "a dunce," and the phrase "hasn't got a clue" followed him around the office.

A few weeks after Napoleon left I was chatting with my wife's Uncle Pete, a retired plumber living on the south side. Pete, a lifelong *Journal* subscriber, asked, "Did the editor leave voluntarily, or was he forced out?" I couldn't look at Pete. I thought of Abraham Lincoln's words: "You can fool all the people some of the time . . ." All that effort the editor spent in putting a spin on his departure and he didn't fool a wily Milwaukee plumber for a minute.

Sure, editors, let's use our newspapers as public relations sheets and arse-covering machines for ourselves. But then let's not be surprised when our credibility with our readers goes down so fast it gets the bends. It's OK to congratulate ourselves when we deserve it. We do that all the time. But we are journalists, dammit. Our readers are not stupid. When we screw up, we should fess up. It wouldn't have hurt for the editor to say something like, "Some of the plans I had for *the Journal* did not turn out as I had hoped," especially the new design. Sadly, Napoleon was not a journalist at heart, but a public relations man, and he was his No. 1 client.

This is not to say that any other editor could have saved the *Journal*. With better leadership, the paper perhaps could have hung on long enough to get a peek at the 21st century. And certainly it would have left a prettier corpse.

The managing editor carried on as executive editor until June, 1993, when the Uppers chose as Napoleon's successor Mary Jo Meisner, forty-one, an Illinois native who had been the managing editor of the *Fort Worth* (Texas) *Star Telegram*. She would be the first woman editor of the *Journal* and its last editor. The new managing editor, who came aboard in February 1994, was Marty Kaiser, late of the *Baltimore Sun*. Both were pleasant and approachable.

With the new regime came what I call "the Cheka." The Cheka was the special force Lenin created in 1918 to assassinate the Romanoff family and it was the forerunner of the notorious KGB. The Cheka would begin work shortly.

In meetings with the staff of the Entertainment Department, Mary Jo became an implacable foe of the Green Sheet. She thought it was old-fashioned—which is precisely what gave it its charm—and she wanted to kill it. The Green Sheet did pose production problems. The pressroom always had to make sure it had an ample supply of green newsprint around, the green paper was expensive, and sometimes it was difficult to obtain paper with a consistent color. The Green Sheet also was an ad-trap. It always ran four pages, so after all the stories, the funnies and features there was chronically limited space for ads. My suggestion was to print the Green Sheet on regular newsprint, but with green ink. That way it could be expanded or contracted with ease and still maintain its green personality.

But Mary Jo was adamant, and so, one sad day in the summer of 1994 the Green Sheet was murdered. Gerald Kloss came out of retirement to write the obit. The Green Sheet had been part of the *Journal* since before World War I. It was discontinued in 1917–18 because of the wartime newsprint shortage, but was resurrected after that and had been part of the paper since.

We tried to take the death as lightly as possible. I stopped at a fabric store and bought some Green Sheet-colored cloth. We made armbands of this and wore them on the Green Sheet's last day. But it was a sad time. Was the Green Sheet killed to prepare the presses for a merged *Journal* and *Sentinel*? Probably.

The Cheka fired its first shot in October, 1994. I got a call from Eric Meyer, the former news systems editor and a close friend. "Well, I am no longer an employee of Journal Communications," he said. What? He said he had been taken down to an office on the third floor where he was . . . um . . . liquidated. He had been with the *Journal* fifteen years. His firing sent a shudder through the news room. They CAN fire you. And they can do it swiftly and brutally.

I am sure there must be a business school course called "Merger 30a," in which companies learn how to push through mergers. We were becoming the victims of some sort of psychological corporate warfare.

The Cheka struck en masse a month later. In what came to be called "The Thanksgiving Week Massacre," 15 people in the advertising department were summarily dismissed—and by "summarily" I mean they weren't allowed to go back to their desks to retrieve their belongings, although I understand many of them did. I knew some of these people, met them in the cafeteria, and I can still see their faces. Among them were Colleen Hiebing, Scott Bong, Dave Emmerich, Phil Esche, Tom Gigere, Carolyn Ziarek, John Hoek, Mark Daniels and Bill Hobday. Another group left voluntarily: Howie Hoerl, Corrine Machula, Ken Nogarski, Scott Stollberg, Phil Marks and Jane Dillon.

This firing had all of us shaking. Now we knew they not only could fire you individually, but in large groups.

Dick Lutz, my mole in the advertising department, said some of the fired people were among the best in the department. Why, then, were they dismissed? There was talk that some of these people were trying to bring a union into the ad department, and management wanted to put a halt to that. Some of these firees got jobs at Community Newspapers Inc., a suburban chain, and were cruelly fired again when Journal Communications bought that company.

By now talk of merging the *Journal* and *Sentinel* was rampant. The only question was "when." Mark Belling, conservative talk-show host on radio station WISN, probably fed by the Uppers, predicted that the merger announcement was imminent. Journalists began to question the Uppers about it. The Uppers would neither confirm nor deny the reports.

Then it was announced that *The Milwaukee Journal*'s News Room Seminar would be held in December that year. In the past it had been held in February or March, so why the change? Well, perhaps because there might not be a *Journal* in February or March.

The seminar, held at the Marquette University Student Union, was a somber affair. The evening's entertainment consisted, in part, of poetry reading!

After the seminar some of us visited one of the local watering holes with Managing Editor Marty Kaiser to drink beer and shoot pool. (I like managing editors who shoot pool with the peons.) We kept asking him "the question"—are we going to merge, and when? All Marty would say was, "Anything can happen in this business."

"Anything" happened on Tuesday afternoon, January 17, 1995. Our editors gathered us in the center of the news room and announced that the *Journal* and *Sentinel* would merge to form the *Journal* (no hyphen) *Sentinel*, a morning paper. The paper would debut on Sunday, March 31.

I shrugged. I had planned to work until sixty, three years away. But I decided then that I would take early retirement and leave peacefully, a company man to the last—at least as far as the *Journal* employee-ownership plan was concerned.

But what of the other people? I looked around me. There weren't going to be enough retirements or voluntary departures to satisfy this merger. I felt especially bad for those in their late forties and early fifties who had many years in but could not take an official retirement at age fifty-five and now would have to try their luck in an uncertain job market. And I sympathized with the younger people, who would be forced to scramble for work elsewhere, and have to leave Milwaukee to do so. It was like the sinking of the *Titanic.* There would not be enough lifeboats for all.

I tried to make light of it, and I certainly could, since my situation was totally secure. With *Journal* stock and other investments, I would be retiring with an increase in income. I bought a "short-timer's chain," something I picked up from the Navy. It was a bead chain with the number of beads representing the days I had left. Each day I would clip a bead from the chain, and in a showy mini-ceremony, place the bead in a dish on my desk. And I bought a sweatshirt and had "AMF—3-31-95" printed on it. I wore this to work. People would ask, "What does the AMF stand for?" I said, "It means 'Adios, My Friends.'" (Heh)

Although the announcement had been expected, it left the newsroom shaking. The moment of truth was here, and it was hard to deal with. The merger was ten weeks away, and we still had two newspapers to put out. It was a very trying period. I was especially proud of our mid-level bosses, such as Beth Slocum in the Features Department. Beth got the distracted and shaken staffers focused on getting the paper out, not knowing whether she would be picked up. (She wasn't. The fools!)

About two weeks after the announcement, our editors gathered us in groups to cross the Rhine (the alley separating the *Journal* and *Sentinel* newsrooms) and visit our separated brethren at the *Sentinel*. The *Sentinel* news room was a dark, dungeon-like place, made so by diffusers placed on the fluorescent lights to keep the glare off the computer screens. Compared to the bright, cheery *Journal* news room, the *Sentinel*'s was like a coal mine. I brought along a box of tissues in case anyone had any ideas about crying. No one did.

I knew a number of *Sentinel*ites, and found them to be . . . um . . . reasonably civil sorts. We eyed each other suspiciously, wondering who was going to find lifeboats, who not.

Some staffers began finding jobs on their own. Rock critic Thor Christensen got a job in Cleveland. Dom Noth, entertainment editor, lined up something else in town. A suburban reporter got a job in Green Bay. But others hung on, hoping to be saved. Each day a staffer or two would get the word—picked up, not picked up.

With about three weeks to Merger Day, there were about twenty positions left to be filled and forty-five people to fill them. The final decision on the staffing of the new *Journal Sentinel* was made in one day. I sat on a copy desk with an editor from the picture desk to watch this sad event.

One by one our colleagues would be called down to the third floor. Minutes later, a door next to the elevators would open and a staffer would emerge. He would stand there, arms outstretched in a helpless gesture, and tilt his head as if to say, sorry, I didn't make it, as though it were his fault. Then the door would open again, and another staffer would emerge and rush into the newsroom, un-smiling. Picked up, but disgusted with the procedure. This went on and on.

We were all wondering what was going to happen to Joel McNally, the witty, liberal author of the column "The Innocent Bystander." We thought the merged paper might assume a more conservative posture, and that Joel would not be a part of it. All eyes were on Joel as he went to the third floor to learn his fate.

The door opened and Joel emerged. He stood there a moment and shook his head. No. He walked into the news room and gathered near the picture desk with a group of friends and supporters to discuss his next move. McNally would have more plots up his sleeve than Guy Fawkes.

More staffers went through the door and down to the third floor. And they came back and made the gestures. Picked up. Not picked up. Then the rejects packed their things and left. One by one, they slowly walked out, our co-workers, our friends, our drinking buddies. My friend's head dropped and he began to cry. "I can't take this anymore," he said.

Our world had ended.

The toll was huge. Mid-level management got flat-tened. Beth was out. So was Dan Chabot, the wonderful Green Sheet editor. Also let go was Jim Slocum, Beth's husband, who was an assistant managing editor at the *Sentinel*.

Also cast out were Marta Bender, another assistant managing editor at the *Sentinel*, and Tom Barber, *Journal* news editor, and Jim Landers, the *Journal*'s Ozaukee-Washington editor, and Tom Mueller, Badger Plus editor, and Dave Staats, *Sentinel* state editor, and Paul Salsini, the *Journal*'s writing coach.

Also leaving, some of them voluntarily, some not, were *Journal* copy editors Mary Fran Cahill, Jim Cattey, Howard Goldfinger, Joy Krause, Don Lewis, Becky Williams, John Wells and yours truly, as well as the *Sentinel*'s wire editor, Pat Rueter. Also dumped were part-time editors Pat Raab and Peggy Schulz of the *Journal* and Charlene Mills of the *Sentinel*.

Gone were *Sentinel* artist Jim Forrest, *Journal* artists Lori Rondinelli, Betsy Behrens and Gene Gerbasi, *Sentinel* photographers Allan Scott and Richard Brodzeller, *Journal* photographers George Cassidy and Jack Orton, *Journal* graphics technician Lynn Howell and *Journal* picture editor Mary Scheffel.

Let go also were *Sentinel* writers Jay Joslyn, Dianne Greening, and Nancy Raabe, *Journal* writers Don Bluhm, Mike Drew, Jackie Gray, Mary Hanson, Paul Hayes and Bill Nelson and part-time feature writer Edith Brin.

Also cast out were Larry Engel and Kathleen Waterbury of the *Sentinel* business desk and Dave Bednarek, Millie Freese and Erik Gunn from the *Journal* business desk. Also, *Journal* writers Jeff Browne, Tyler Chin, Cynthia Dennis, Mark Edmund, Phil Nero and Mike Krenn.

Going down with the ship were part-time reporters, Jamaal Abdul-Alim of the *Sentinel* and Tom Cioni, Anne Davis, Nancy Johnson, Stan McCoy, Dave Thome and Carol Wahlen of the *Journal*.

From the *Sentinel* sports department went Bud Lea, Ken Bunch, Terry Koper, and part-timer Steve Bruss. Also out were Pat Stiegman of Badger Plus and Adam Mertz, a part-timer there.

Editorial assistants Jan Basina of the *Journal* and Josette Cohen of the *Sentinel* were cut, as were part-time assistants Nancy Beatty from the *Sentinel*'s Madison Bureau and Tracy Harris and Kristina Knapcik of the *Sentinel* news room.

Clerical people and newsroom helpers terminated were Rick Geise, John Kizenkavich, Clarice Kroening, Barbara Pleva, Chris Reed, Jennifer Shillinglaw, Ella White and Brenda Wolfer and part-timers Lisa Polacheck and Tony Punko, all of the *Journal*, and June Dzemske, Debbie Harings, Terry Olson, and Darlene Wimberly of the *Sentinel*.

The News Information Center (I liked it better when they called that place the Morgue) ousted Jo Reitman, its manager, and Angie Alexander, Larry Ill, Heather Marshall-Gergen, Lillian Schultz and Marie Spoern.

We had a huge farewell party for *Journal* staffers at Turner Hall, north of The Journal building. Everyone got a chance to take the podium and offer a brief statement. Under normal circumstances these people would have had their own going-away parties, with speeches, gag gifts, roasts, toasts, perhaps a poem. Now they were just dumped, en masse. Most of them I never saw again.

There was a lot of anger among journalists who had wanted to continue their careers, but instead were told that, after all their years of work for the paper, they were no longer wanted. I think JournalComm management failed to deal properly with this anger. It would pay for that.

21

Aftermath

The merged *Journal Sentinel* came with a completely new design. A cacophony of typography, it was not much of an improvement over the previous design. It was like opening your front door and having sixteen children come rushing in demanding attention at once. The stretched-out M I L W A U K E E over the logo looked like something we used to do in the fifth grade. I thought the best design was the one that existed before the disastrous redesign of 1990.

The Uppers were irrationally exuberant about the prospects of a merged paper. Prior to the merger, a promotional film was shown at the Performing Arts Center downtown. The new design was praised and the Uppers said they were shooting for a *Journal Sentinel* circulation of 400,000 daily and 600,000 Sunday. By the spring of 2002 daily circulation was 249,000 and Sunday circulation 434,000.

With the merger, Journal Communications got a new chairman of the board, Joel McNally. Or so it seemed.

When the merger went through, those of us over 55 could take official retirement and thus have 10 years to sell our stock back, 10% of the units per year, thereby spreading out our capital gains tax liabilities. But we wondered what would happen to the people under 55, many of whom had considerable amounts of stock. Certainly the company would not force them to sell all their stock at once. Then word drifted down that most of these people would have five years to sell their stock back. To me, this meant they would sell their stock back in five parcels, 20 percent of the units each year.

But the Uppers, who were having one of their bad months, failed to explain this. Instead, the they said these five-year people could sell their units "within" five years, which could be interpreted to mean that they could hang onto their stock for five years then sell all the units at once.

Thanks to a terrible lawsuit the company lost a few years earlier, the price of *Journal* stock was depressed. The suit involved an alleged patent infringement by one of JournalComm's printing plants in New England. One report has it that the suit could have been settled out of court for a mere $75,000 (another source said $750,000), but that the Uppers decided to fight it. Then some important documents turned up missing, someone insulted the judge handling the case, and a suit that could have been settled for $75,000 (or $750,000) ended up costing the company $22.4 million. Because of this lawsuit, *Journal* stock for several years was producing total returns in the area of 7.5%, rather than the usual 15%.

The price of *Journal* stock historically has been set by a rather involved formula involving accounting periods, earnings and costs and other figures. Since the stock was not publicly traded, it was difficult to determine its true value. But if you compared the price/earnings ratio of JournalComm with that of other communications companies, Journal stock was grossly undervalued. If the company chose to go public with its stock, I do believe there would be a stampede of buyers.

McNally struck his first blow in 1996 when he found a man named Christopher Shaw, a New York investment banker, who reportedly had a buyer standing in the wings willing to pay $1 billion for Journal Communications. (In addition to owning the *Milwaukee Journal Sentinel*, Journal Communications owns Milwaukee's WTMJ TV and WTMJ radio stations, WKTI FM, a batch of radio and TV stations around the country, a cable service company, a group of shoppers, a fiber optic company, printing plants and a marketing company.)

McNally—and a lot of others—argued that the company had a "fiduciary responsibility" to explore Shaw's offer. A lot of others—including myself—were loudly opposed to selling the company because this would destroy the employee-ownership plan.

The company reacted in part to the Shaw thing (though it didn't say as much) by revamping the formula for pricing the stock. It created a "ramp-up" that would push the stock price closer to the price/earnings ratios of other communications companies. The ramp-up would begin in 1997 and run through 2001.

The ramp-up formula broke the teeth of the Shaw challenge. But never underestimate the wiliness of a columnist suffering from *careerus interruptus*. McNally struck again.

McNally took on the "within five years" sellback statement. He rounded up 152 people and hired a law firm to sue the company over this issue.

Because of the way the "within" was incorporated into the company's statement, the over-55 retirees could become part of the suit. I refused to join. I could see where the company erred in spelling out the sellback procedures. But in order to accept the plaintiffs' argument, one would have to believe that JournalComm suddenly, deliberately and without warning changed the traditional sellback procedure and now was reneging on these changes.

I thought the company could have escaped this thing with a swift "Setting It Straight." But it allowed the matter to fester and then get into court, where JournalComm has had as much good fortune as Susan Lucci seeking an Emmy.

While the suit was pending, Tom Pavek, my mole in the Production Department and a retiree who was part of the suit, called me and asked how many units (shares) of stock I owned when I retired. I told him. He broke out his calculator and said that—judging by the settlement figures then being bandied about—I had just thrown away $286,018.

The suit was settled in the spring of 2002. The plaintiffs would share $8.9 million. By not taking part in the suit, I had thrown away a mere $28,000.

It was all very sad. Since *Journal* stock is closely held—only active employees and retirees and original owners can hold it—a dispute resembles a family squabble over money. And now outside lawyers were brought in to sup at our table. Very sad.

But it was—thank God!—over with.

22

Epilogue

Some people feel that newspapers are passe, that in a few years people will be getting their news strictly from TV, radio and the Internet. I don't believe that.

The difficulty with TV, radio and the Internet is that they operate in a medium of time, while newspapers operate in a medium of space. You can spend only twenty-four hours in front of a TV set, or listening to the radio or surfing the Internet. But you can produce a newspaper that could take seven or more days to read. A newspaper can be an omnibus, carrying stories and information that only 5 percent of its readers will want to know.

Newspapers have the advantage of portability and permanence—you can carry them with you and you can clip things from them. And one paper can be separated into parts and read by a group of people at once. The family can grab the Sunday *Journal Sentinel* and head for the park, where Mom reads the Lifestyle section, Dad reads the Sports section, and the kiddies read the Business section. A formidable mode of communication. I think newspaper readership may decline some because of competition with other media, but I can't see the day when newspapers aren't with us. And as advertising machines, newspapers are truly awesome.

The *Milwaukee Journal Sentinel*, in its professionalism, fairness and completeness, is a damned good newspaper. There are blunders, of course, such as its slowness in picking up on the Milwaukee County Board pension fiasco. But its handling of the 2000 presidential election was a shining example of fairness—almost fastidiously so—and its use of the Op Ed page allows us to temper our political views with those of others.

Much is made of bias in our business. There is supposed to be this beast called "the liberal media." I have seen biased papers in the past, but I would argue that today the news media are essentially neutral. I love those TV programs on which issues are aired and viewers are invited to call in using different phone numbers if they are a Republican, Democrat, or Independent/Other.

The "liberal media" charge comes mainly from the right-wing ideologues we hear on radio. But ideologues, whether of the right or left, are first cousins of the lunatic fringe, and journalists have great difficulty dealing with them because they feel that such people are . . . um . . . tetched.

When I was working for the *Chicago Tribune*, a liberal friend of mine suggested that I must be under some pressure to bias stories to the right, that there must at the very least be a "When in Rome do as the Romans do" influence over my work. Well, perhaps a little, especially among young and impressionable journalists. I once got scolded by Larry Fein for tilting a headline too far to the right. And the *Tribune* certainly was a mecca for conservative journalists. But the *Tribune* never asked me to bias anything, and if it had I wouldn't have done so. However, I cannot vouch for what happened at the *Tribune* during the Colonel McCormick era.

It is true, of course, that most journalists are—politically—liberal, just as most surgeons are—politically—conservative. But to what extent do these professionals inject their political views into their work? Do journalists who happen to be politically liberal sabotage news favorable to conservatives? Do surgeons who happen to be politically conservative suture politically liberal patients with less care than they would suture politically conservative patients? Check your abdominal scars!

Conservatives, the way I see them, come in three types: There are progressive conservatives, of whom Teddy Roosevelt would be a good example. Then constructive conservatives like John McCain. And finally status quo or regressive conservatives such as Phyllis Schlafly. (If Colonel McCormick had been cloned, and the cloners didn't mind crossing the sex barrier, they probably would have ended up with Phyllis Schlafly.)

It is the Schlafly types who have difficulty getting a favorable press. The working-mother journalist is going to have a problem warming up to Schlafly, who believes that women (excepting herself) should stay home and have babies and make fudge and that rape victims impregnated by their attackers should be denied abortions. So, yes, people who take extreme positions well out of mainstream political thinking might have a hard time getting good press.

But Ronald (Teflon Ron) Reagan certainly got good press. Dick Cheney, during the 2000 election campaign, was asked if he had any complaints about the way his campaign was covered. He shook his head no. John F. Kennedy got a good press, and that was partly because, like Reagan, he was a delightful personality. Nixon did not get a good press; Willy Sutton didn't either. (Willy was a bank robber).

If you look at the coverage of the presidents of the 20th century you will find that those who got the best press were those who had the most appealing personalities, their politics be damned.

There is a group called Accuracy in Media (AIM), which complains that conservative viewpoints do not get a proper airing in the media. But the more one explores AIM's complaints the more one finds that AIM is not complaining so much about a biased media, but that the media are not kissing AIM's arse. The media shouldn't kiss anybody's arse. Journalists should place a steel ring around themselves and drop a "not for sale" sign on it. I think that is exactly what journalists do.

All journalists should be Voltaire people: "I may not agree with what you have to say, but I will defend to the death your right to say it." Again, I think most journalists are.

I feel that journalism USA has never been more responsible, fair or open-minded in its history. Journalists, my favorite people, do absolutely marvelous work.

An article in *USA Today* quoted a journalist who said that to show his lack of bias he refused to vote in national elections. Come on! If you haven't got your biases potty-trained no amount of non-voting is going to remedy your situation.

We journalists need not fear our political, religious or social beliefs, no matter how strongly we hold them. What we journalists MUST fear is our failure to live up to the standards of our profession. And we know what those standards are: Get it and get it right, get both sides, respect the viewpoints of others—and don't slug any stories "Unwashed."